LEAN INNOVATION GUIDE

A Proven Approach for Innovation Success

DAVID GRIESBACH

BIS Publishers

BIS Publishers
Borneostraat 80-A
1094 CP Amsterdam
The Netherlands
T +31 (0)20 515 02 30
bis@bispublishers.com
www.bispublishers.com

ISBN 978 90 636966 8 9

Book design & graphics:
Christian Heusser, Roman Schnyder
and Fabienne Vuilliomenet,
Equipo GmbH Basel www.equipo.ch

Image credit:
Equipo GmbH, Pexels, Pixabay

English translation:
Karen Caruana

To my wife Samira,
our daughters Léa and Olive,
and my parents who have
always believed in me.

*Very early in my career at the age of 23, I was given the responsibility
of developing a web-based solution for the execution of customer
projects at one of Switzerland's biggest communication agencies. The
request had come from one of our main clients, a Swiss subsidiary
of a global telecommunications provider. The company wanted to be
able to collaborate independent of time and place, and also access
the project history at any time. Naturally, our project team first spoke
at great length with users, both within our agency, and also with
our clients, to define the requirements and specifications. For approximately 50,000 euros we had external software programmers
develop a solution that met the identified requirements in every respect.
Projects could be set up for users with different access rights, and
the type of notifications and their frequency could be customized for
each user. Just like today's social media channels, each project
and its communication history was posted chronologically on a "news
wall" of sorts, thus ensuring constant transparency.*

*How did the users react? Neither the client's users nor our
consultants ever used the solution. The whole thing was a total failure.
And for me personally, it was a very disappointing experience.
Why did the client want the solution and then end up not using it,
after all that? Had we not understood what exactly would
have provided the desired added value? And how could I have better
managed the project? Should we have had even more discussions
with the potential users? Should they have been even more involved
in the development, and more consistently? Over the next few
years, these unanswered questions and so many more kept going
through my head...*

… until I met the inventor of the Business Model Canvas, Alex Osterwalder, in 2011. He invited me to one of his first master classes, at which point I became aware of the Lean Startup movement. It immediately became clear to me that the Lean approach would resolve my long unanswered questions regarding the unsuccessful extranet project, and that Lean Startup would unleash a transformation that would overhaul innovation management from the ground up.

Extreme uncertainty as a challenge in the innovation process
In the case of innovative products and services, the challenge lies in the fact that as developers, we always believe we're creating an added value that will be seen as such by potential customers. But because innovations inevitably entail wide-ranging modifications—for example, due to new solutions for existing or new problems, new user behavior or new distribution channels—there's really no way for us to know in advance if and how the desired added value will actually be identified by the customers. The Lean approach has found a better way of dealing with this extreme uncertainty.

Lean Startup and related approaches have thus laid the foundation for the paradigm shift needed in startup and innovation management. At around the same time, I was already working on developing a similar approach as part of my PhD thesis. With this in mind, I immediately saw the potential of Lean Startup. From this point forward, I dedicated myself to the topic and have since committed myself to Lean as a ground-breaking approach to innovation management.

Lean Innovation instead of Lean Startup
In this book, I will be using the term Lean Innovation and I refer to any innovation processes and activities being conducted according to the Lean approach described here, whether in a startup, a SME or a corporation.

While Lean Startup finds its origins in the startup scene, it not only
depicts how startups come to be but also describes a generally
new approach to developing innovative businesses, products and
services. The term "Lean Innovation" also includes all closely
associated methods such as customer development[1], running Lean[2],
agile innovation management or related concepts.

Extreme uncertainty openly acknowledged

The Lean approach openly acknowledges the extreme uncertainty
around innovation projects and innovative startups, whereas
traditionally, the business plan would try to get a handle on uncertainty
through planning that was as accurate as possible. The innovation
process according to Lean Innovation concedes from the outset
that in most cases, the original innovation idea will have to be changed
to guarantee market success. Quite a few innovation projects
even have to be abandoned so that the limited resources can be implemented for new, much more promising ideas. The earlier a change
in direction or the necessity to end the project is identified, the leaner
our process is.

Unknown assumptions as the basis for experimentation

Lean Innovation has also recognized that innovation projects are based
on a multitude of assumptions. For example, we assume that
customers are not fully satisfied with the previous solutions, or that
potential customers get their information through a specific
media channel and we can use that channel to promote our innovation.
The assumptions depict smaller and larger risks that have to be
prioritized. Thanks to prioritization, the largest risks and their underlying assumptions can first be tested, namely through experimentation
such as interviews with potential customers, an initial website
to collect e-mail addresses, or a prototype. With the help of prioritization, which also requires continuous testing and adapting, the

innovation process becomes extremely agile and lean because we only invest the minimum in order to learn what is next-most important or represents the highest risk. This process lets us gradually advance towards genuine added value for potential customers and thus the success of the innovation project. In the traditional planning process, the potential customer's decision remains unpredictable right up to the very end, thus representing a considerable risk. Thanks to experimentation, Lean Innovation allows us to identify the route to an innovation project that satisfies potential customers and will thus also be financially successful.

Worldwide Lean Innovation transformation in the works

The Lean approach is already being implemented in the startup and entrepreneur world, but corporations have also started to align themselves to these new paradigms of innovation management. These include, in Switzerland, companies like Swisscom, AXA Versicherungen and Rivella, and in Germany, companies like Lufthansa, Kärcher and Sennheiser. But global companies like General Electric, Proctor & Gamble, Google and Dropbox have also been using Lean Innovation for several years now.[3] Because this is truly a fundamentally new form of innovating, companies and staff are still considerably challenged by this transformation. And many small and medium-sized businesses haven't even started to develop innovative products and services using the Lean approach. We thus find ourselves on the threshold of this transformation.

In the traditional planning process, the customer's decision remains
unpredictable right up to the very end.

INTRODUCTION

HOW WILL YOU BENEFIT FROM THIS BOOK?

I promise that the benefits you derive from this book will be two-fold. First, to date, there is no compact and clearly structured summary of the key ideas, models and tools applied in the Lean Innovation approach. The first part delivers on that promise. If you're new to Lean Innovation or still don't know everything about it, this first part is the perfect foundation and a great introduction. If you're already an expert, you can look up specific topics or use the book to refresh your memory. In addition to defining Lean Innovation, the first chapter explains the key ideas and models. This is followed by a detailed explanation of why Lean is the right approach for innovative startups and innovation management in a company. The first part ends with a toolbox that succinctly introduces the most widely-used tools.

Consolidation of the most important Lean Innovation books, models and tools

Second, you'll have the Lean Progress Model at your fingertips. This new tool will allow you to efficiently introduce and successfully implement the Lean Innovation approach. In the traditional process, we stuck to the business plan, which promised safety and clarity, even if only outwardly. By contrast, Lean Innovation requires that we go through an open-ended exploration and learning process. For this, we need a guide that shows us the process or the current status of a startup or innovation project at a glance. To date, there has been no such guide, and this is exactly what the Lean Progress Model delivers. It consists of the six key success factors of a startup or innovation project. The associated guiding questions help direct the process and the stoplight colors indicate the current status based on interactions and experimentation conducted with potential customers.

The model is explained in depth in the second part using the six success factors. Each factor has its own chapter explaining the key thoughts in detail, supplemented with helpful models and methods. Each chapter ends with the success factor's key guiding questions and a helpful tool so you can choose the right stoplight color. The third part shows you how you can optimally apply the Lean Progress Model and properly synchronize it with the company-specific processes. Using a concrete example, I demonstrate how the Lean Progress Model helped a customer avoid unnecessary investments and develop true added value in a very short time. In conclusion, the model serves as a structure that allows individuals, teams and organizations to assess the model with respect to the preferred success factor. Seven different innovation templates can be identified.

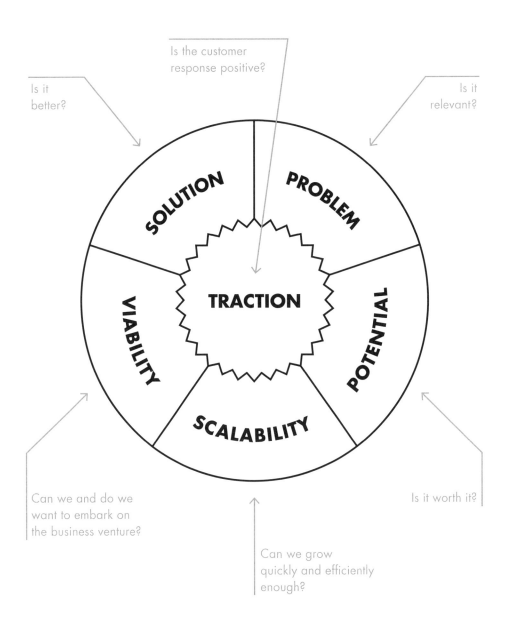

The Lean Progress Model for successfully implementing Lean Innovation

HOW DOES A LEAN PROGRESS MODEL IMPROVE THE SUCCESS OF YOUR STARTUP OR INNOVATION?

In the hundred or so startup or innovation projects I've had the privilege of supporting using the Lean Innovation approach, it became clear to me that many users are struggling with this new approach to innovation. We are so trained and taught to use analyses that are as precise as possible when we theoretically forecast and plan how a project should go, that a gradual forward-looking approach to exploration and learning is something we still need to internalize. As worthwhile and important as Lean Innovation is, applying it brings its own challenges, which need to be mastered:

1. Without a business plan, there needs to be an alternate transparent <u>focus</u> as to where we currently find ourselves in the open-ended learning process.

2. The open process can result in people getting lost in the many opportunities. That is why a strong <u>focus</u> and <u>prioritization</u> are fundamental to operating in a manner that is truly lean.

3. Lack of <u>speed</u> is another key source of waste in the innovation process. We have to test the most important assumptions as quickly as possible and derive the necessary modifications based on this.

The Lean Innovation models and tools developed up to this point have not yet been able to adequately solve these key challenges. This is exactly where the Lean Process Model is applied. The six success factors of an innovation project provide direction and make it clear as to all the things you need to pay attention to and where you currently are in the exploration and learning process. Thanks to the guiding questions, you know exactly what needs to be tested, and in what order.

In addition, the color scheme helps you assess a project in as little time as possible and to plan the next development steps using the evaluation. In summary, the Lean Progress Model helps you introduce a <u>maximum amount of transparency, focus and speed</u> to your startup and innovation projects so that there is no longer anything standing in the way of success.

WHO IS THE BOOK AND THE MODEL MEANT FOR, AND HOW SHOULD THEY BE USED?

Essentially, the book and the model are directed at anyone who deals with innovative business opportunities, products and services and, more generally, with added value for customers and users. The book and the model will support you in a variety of ways:

– Above all else, Lean Innovation is intended to make and keep businesses and organizations <u>successful in the long term</u>, thus avoiding unnecessary investments.

– The Lean Innovation Guide will allow you to develop <u>new business opportunities, products and services</u> that will provide your customers with real added value.

– This book will allow you to quickly and efficiently introduce Lean Innovation as a <u>method and philosophy in your business</u> and to <u>further disseminate</u> it throughout your organization. Anyone who deals with new business opportunities, products and services, and added value for customers, even in the broadest sense, should have and use the Lean Innovation Guide. An investment that pays off, many times over.

– The progress model allows you to better manage the innovation process according to Lean principles, to <u>identify process progress within seconds</u>, and to transparently communicate this to various stakeholders.

- This gives you the tools you need to <u>dramatically increase innovation speed</u> and considerably shorten the time it takes to achieve success.

- It's not just about that big "innovation design." The Lean Progress Model helps you <u>strictly maintain user and value direction</u>, even for less extensive product improvements and new functionality, as well as internal optimization.

- In terms of <u>education and further education</u>, the Lean Innovation Guide provides you with a condensed introduction to Lean Innovation methods, which is very much appreciated by participants. If your role is to support and coach innovation projects, you'll find the process of following the Lean Progress Model extremely transparent and coherent.

- The points above demonstrate that the Lean Innovation Guide and the Lean Progress Model are beneficial to people in a wide variety of roles within a company and other organizations: <u>CEOs, executives, department heads, strategists, innovation managers and their teams, research and development staff, product managers, business developers, software and hardware engineers, startup founders, contractors, consultants, trainers and lecturers.</u>

HOW IS THE BOOK DESIGNED?

The title says it all: it's designed as a pocket guide or coach, a handbook to accompany you along every step of implementing a Lean Innovation approach. The book is meant to help you navigate a development and innovation process that is often unpredictable. For this reason, I opted for a very specific structure: individual topics, ideas, models or tools are printed on facing pages or across four pages. An associated image provides additional clarification for the text on the facing page, but is also meant to stimulate thought and reflection.

LEAN INNOVATION: INTRODUCTION

WHAT IS LEAN INNOVATION?

PAGE 32

DEFINITION: LEAN INNOVATION IS

THROUGH **CONTINUOUS DEVELOPMENT**

OR REJECTS THE **MARKET VIABILITY**

AS QUICKLY AND AS

PAGE 42

PAGE 38

PAGE 40

PAGE 26

AN **INNOVATION PROCESS**,* THAT

TESTING AND **OPTIMIZING, PROVES**

PAGE 36

PAGE 34

OF AN INNOVATION IDEA

EAN AS POSSIBLE.

FOR AN EXPLANATION OF THE KEY IDEAS AND MODELS, GO TO THE INDICATED PAGES FOR EACH OF THE UNDERLINED TERMS.

*also includes innovation methodology, innovation philosophy or an innovation paradigm

U ntil a short time ago, innovations were developed along the three following simplified process steps: (1) First, we would draft a blueprint and write a business plan. (2) Then we would develop and test the actual product or service. (3) And last, the innovation would be launched on the market (see the top image on the facing page).

The issue with this method is that we think we know from the outset where this innovation train will take us. We more or less blindly believe that our idea is so certain to provide our potential customers with added value that they will definitely be interested in it and will pay for the offering. Unfortunately, it's not until later in the process that we know whether or not this is the case.

THE INNOVATION PROCESS

Until now, we assumed that if we analyzed the innovation idea closely enough at the outset using the business plan, we would eliminate or at least minimize the risk of failure. There are many counterarguments to challenge this assumption: First, many in-novation ideas change over the course of the process, sometimes even substantially, which makes the original plan void. Second, the financial projections are, for the most part, fictional and based on many unquestioned assumptions. And third, we end up investing a lot of time and money into the project before we finally find out if the customers are ready to pay for it. This results in sunk costs, and the project contents might be changed a little or a lot, or the project might even be canceled.

THE TRADITIONAL INNOVATION PROCESS

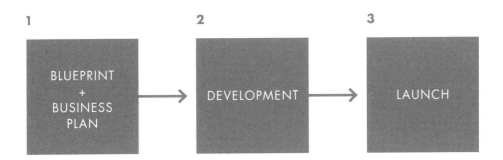

THE INNOVATION PROCESS ACCORDING TO LEAN STARTUP

The Lean Innovation process compared to the traditional innovation process

Although the traditional process has the right intention of wanting to minimize the risk of failure, many innovation and startup projects fail when they're launched because the original plan was hypothetical and delusional.[4] Now and then in the startup world, this poor track record would be the decisive factor in the formation of a new approach using Lean Innovation. The idea behind the three new phases can be summarized as follows[5] (see bottom image on page 27):

PHASE 1: PROBLEM-SOLUTION FIT

The added value recognized by the potential customer is in the foreground. Only if the solution solves a customer's specific problem and the solution is better than previous alternatives can the innovation achieve true added value, which corresponds to a problem-solution fit.

PHASE 2: PRODUCT-MARKET FIT

In order to be a product-market fit, enough potential customers have to be interested in and prepared to pay for the new offering. In other words, in this case, there is an actual market for the innovation. In addition, we have to be able to operate the business at a profit, which means that the product and the business model are viable.

PHASE 3: SCALABILITY

Even if we're able to prove the existence of a market and the viability of our business idea, we still don't know with certainty if we can grow with enough efficiency and speed. In other words, we assess whether the business can be grown sufficiently.

As opposed to the traditional innovation process, we're no longer trying to get a handle on risk from the outset through planning that is as accurate as possible; rather, we continuously minimize the risks. We acknowledge that an idea only represents an initial assumption, that the idea's market viability will have to be tested and improved, and that because of this, the idea itself will change.

Plus, the process is no longer linear because, after every phase, we have to be really critical in our analysis of whether or not the fit was actually achieved. Without a true fit, we have to either make additional changes to the project or shelve it altogether in order to use the scarce time and financial resources for even better projects.

Because we pause after every step to really critically assess whether we can and should continue, it's better to talk about phases than process steps. Many organizations are not used to changing a project early on in the process or even shelving it. But the more we develop a project in the wrong direction, the more expensive it will be to change directions later on, plus it might be a market failure.

As an alternative or in combination with the three-step process, the four steps of the original approach of Lean Startup are very useful. The so-called Customer Development Process[6] formed the basis of Lean Startup and was developed by serial entrepreneur and university lecturer Steve Blank. He is the founder and father of Lean Startup as a modern form of entrepreneurship.

The first step, "Customer Discovery," is about the customer attitude towards the problem and the need for a solution. Customers see an early version of the product for the first time. In the second step, "Customer Validation," the repeatability and scalability of the business model must be proven, which is necessary for a profitable venture. In the third step, "Customer Creation," the focus is on sales and marketing. Here, for the first time, we step on the gas and spend larger sums on marketing. And only in the fourth step, "Company Building," is the startup transformed into a more established company.

The four-step Customer Development Process of Steve Blank as the
original version of Lean Startup

U nder a Lean approach, the development of innovative products and services is no longer just in the second phase,
as it is in the traditional process, but instead, throughout the
entire innovation process. Development is thus continuous and
corresponds to a cycle consisting of the three steps "develop,"
"measure" and "learn." The goal of this iterative procedure is
to find out as quickly and economically as possible whether the
developed aspects of the idea and its underlying assumptions
will be confirmed or rejected by potential customers.

CONTINUOUS
DEVELOPMENT

The benefit of iterative development is that the development
steps and the related mistakes will be very small, but the learning
effect will be that much greater. Investments by cycle are mini-
mal, as is the risk of failure. Plus, the innovation process will
inevitably be more flexible. After each iteration, an improvement
or pivot can be executed and is also often necessary. Because we
don't know at the outset where this journey will take us, we're in
a better place to find out which step is next, until we can assess
whether we have reached our milestone in the Lean Innovation
process after several cycles.

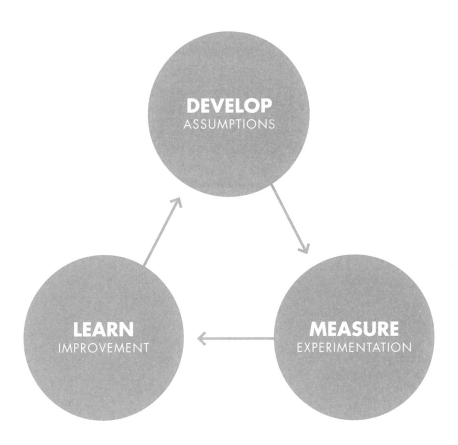

The develop-measure-learn cycle (adapted from Ries, 2014)

I nvolving existing or potential customers as early as possible in the innovation process is one of the most important requirements in the Lean approach. We want to find out as quickly and as lean as possible whether our idea could be successful, whether it needs to be changed, or whether it doesn't stand a chance on the market.

The additional requirement of "as quickly and as lean as possible" helps decide which form of customer interaction makes the most sense, and when. The recommendation is to start by conducting in-depth, qualitative one-on-one interviews, as these represent the quickest and least costly form of interaction and no complex components of the offer need to be developed yet. Once the interviews no longer provide any new insights, we can develop the first prototype. This is usually the case after about thirty to fifty interviews.[7] What is key is that interactions with the customers never fully stop. If the prototype has also played a part in the learning and development process, an initial minimum viable product (MVP) can be developed. An MVP is different from a prototype in that the key benefits of the new MVP can be experienced by the customer and the customers have to pay for the added value.

TESTING

Let's assume we're creating a new weekly shopping service for families. An informative website of the offering would correspond to an initial prototype. However, an MVP would have to make the key benefits of this shopping service tangible, by letting a person run a test on an address they've personally selected, for example.

Testing objective: The assumptions and reactions converge as much as possible

Another, very important requirement in the Lean Innovation process is drawing the right conclusions from the customer interaction and optimizing them respectively. Unfortunately, customers never give us a black and white answer. Their feedback is always gray, so unclear. And yet as innovators, we have to decide on either white or black for every unanswered question. The method here differs between a general change in direction (pivoting) and fine-tuning the idea.[8] A general pivot changes the idea considerably, whereas fine-tuning only optimizes individual elements of the main idea. To recognize the necessary modifications, it is recommended that you take cues from the potential customers' level of enthusiasm. Enthusiasm can be both positive and negative. Strong feelings show us that we're on the trail of an important topic. If potential customers are not emotionally moved by the topics, we can assume they'll never be interested in our offering.

OPTIMIZING

Innovators often get stuck in their first idea and no longer want to change it. They feel obliged to defend their ideas both internally and with customers. But defense is a virtue of the traditional process. Lean Innovation requires a willingness to learn, flexibility, being tolerant of a margin of error, and openness. To promote practices such as this, it's helpful to be aware of your own behavior. In the last chapter, we'll describe seven typical innovation templates that address this.

FINE-TUNING

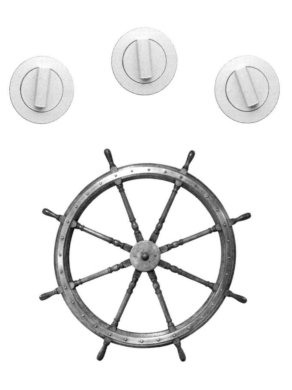

PIVOT

The difference between a general pivot and fine-tuning

A n innovation project is commercially viable when four conditions are met simultaneously. For many projects, this is not the case from the outset. But we use Lean Innovation to try to prove or refute as quickly as possible that all four conditions apply or do not:

1. The innovation idea must address a solvable problem. A solution for an irrelevant problem will never be commercially viable, as the customers aren't even looking for a solution.

2. The new solution has to be better than alternative solutions. Previous solutions can also be very simple, such as "writing down a list." Added value only occurs if the problem is solved in a manner that is significantly better.

MARKET VIABILITY

3. The customers need to map the timeline, have a financial budget for the solution and be willing to use the budget for this and no other solutions or topics. And enough potential buyers for the solution are needed.

4. The customers need to map the timeline, have a financial budget for the solution and be willing to use the budget for this and no other solutions or topics. And enough potential buyers for the solution are needed.[9]

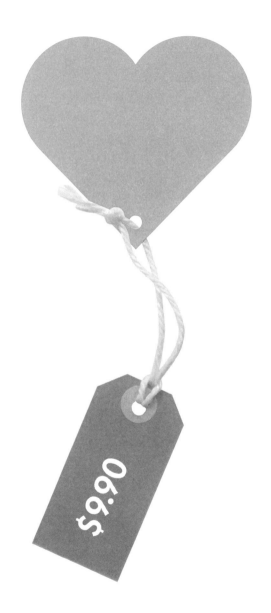

No customer interest or money means no market viability

T he term "Lean" is so important that it needs to be explained once more. It comes from the term "Lean Thinking," which has been applied in production companies using Lean Production or Lean Manufacturing for several decades now. The term "Lean" stands for waste reduction—the elimination of all unnecessary steps in the production process. The final product of production is, however, unlike with the innovation process, known beforehand.

AS QUICKLY AND
AS LEAN AS POSSIBLE

The requirements for innovation are entirely different from those for production. We don't know what the final product will be and find ourselves in an open-ended learning and exploration process to find out which problem can be solved with which new approach. In the investment field, lean refers to omitting high-risk development and marketing investments. We only develop and invest in what is most important in order to test the highest risk assumptions and continuously improve the innovation idea. Time spent must also be seen as an investment. The earlier we know if an idea promises to be successful, the more quickly we can ramp up this idea to market maturity; if the opposite holds true, we need to devote ourselves to a more promising idea. Lean refers to a minimum investment of time and money with a maximum learning effect. At least twelve different forms of waste can be identified in the innovation process.

1. IRRELEVANT PROBLEM
The solution to a problem
that is not important enough

2. IRRELEVANT SOLUTION
There is no value added as compared to
alternative solutions, or it is not high enough

3. RISK-POTENTIAL RELATIONSHIP
The risk of a failure compared to the
potential of success is too high

4. OVERDEVELOPMENT
Effort and functions not yet
required for learning

5. OVERPRODUCTION
Production too high
(if not digital)

6. OVER-ANALYSIS
Too much theoretical work instead of customer
interactions, or the work and learning effect of
customer interactions is disproportionate

7. RISK PRIORITIZATION
Major risks are not prioritized
high enough

8. HIDDEN ASSUMPTIONS
Major risks are
not identified

9. WAIT TIMES
A slowdown in learning speed, whether
self-inflicted or due to external issues

10. FRAGMENTATION
Too many things at the same time,
key development levers not identified

11. PREMATURE SCALING
High investment in distribution, marketing and
sales before the product-market fit was proven

12. USE OF CAPABILITIES
Capabilities not used fully or appropriately;
unimportant activities not outsourced

Twelve types of waste to be avoided in the innovation process

W hen we innovate, we run the risk of focusing on the obvious aspects and assessing them too optimistically. However, in the exploration and learning process according to Lean Innovation, it is essential to be aware of hidden assumptions underlying an innovation idea. For example, if we develop a cutting-edge bicycle, we assume that potential customers are not satisfied with some of the functionalities of currently available bicycles (Assumption 1). Further, we assume that the cutting-edge bicycle cannot easily be copied by the competition (Assumption 2). Assumptions such as these serve as guides for the learning process and prioritization of experimentation. Should we first check whether the idea can be protected by copyright (Assumption 2) or whether the solution even solves an applicable customer problem (Assumption 1)? It is obvious that in this case, we need to start with Assumption 1, because what good is a patent for an idea if it might not even be of interest to potential customers?

PROVE OR REJECT

Start by making a list of assumptions, prioritize them and conduct an exploration and learning process using the prioritized list of assumptions. Formulate the assumptions using the following opening sentence: "We assume that..." Rephrased as a hypothesis, prove or reject each assumption. Naturally, in the process, new assumptions might be added, and previous ones might be eliminated. The order of priority might change, too. The list of assumptions is a continuously changing tool.

OBVIOUS ASPECTS
ASSESSED TOO
POSITIVELY

HIDDEN
ASSUMPTIONS

The biggest risks are found in the hidden assumptions

THE FUTURE
IS LEAN

I magine a scenario where seven out of ten newly constructed homes collapse within five years of being built. You have no idea whether the house in which you might be reading this book, for example, is safe. A rather unpleasant feeling. So unpleasant and, especially, life-threatening, that structural engineers and architects need to quickly figure out which new building technique would prevent this.

THE PARADIGM SHIFT
WAS OVERDUE

Imagine seven out of ten innovation and startup projects are terminated after five years because they're unsuccessful.[10] While this might not be life-threatening, all the time and money invested will be lost, or at least, will not have resulted in any added value. Since the 1950s, innovative companies, founders and researchers have been working hard to improve this poor success rate. However, their focus was always on trying to make an even better plan, rather than questioning the plan itself.[11] It was the Lean approach that finally recognized that we cannot plan with more precision when we're working under conditions of extreme uncertainty, as is the case with innovation projects. Instead, we need to deal with extreme uncertainty differently. The related paradigm shift inevitably needs to challenge a few key assumptions.

FALSE ASSUMPTION 1:
AWESOME IDEA = SUCCESS

There's usually a brilliant individual at the center of publicly cel-
ebrated innovations, someone who has much better and much
more successful ideas. There's a lot of hype behind this person's
creativity and the idea itself. Some ideas might be better, others
might be worse, but even the good ideas first need to prove
themselves in a lengthy and arduous implementation phase. If
we challenge the first assumption, it's no longer about being as
creative as possible and searching for that one, brilliant idea, but
rather, about better guiding the development and implementation process.

FALSE ASSUMPTION 2:
INITIAL IDEA = IMPLEMENTED IDEA

The original idea usually ends up being changed somewhat, but often even extensively. On the surface, certain ideas seem to remain
stable, but in every case, the configuration details change during
implementation. If several businesses are pursuing the same idea,
it's only in the implementation approach that it becomes clear
who is in the lead. Let's look at the example of payment using a
mobile device like a smartphone or a smartwatch. The startup
platform Angel.co lists more than 2,100 businesses that have dedicated efforts towards this idea.[12] It's still unclear which systems
will prevail. But in any case, the main idea won't change. What
will change is the configuration details of the service, the usability, or the way in which the community is built.

FALSE ASSUMPTION 3:
BUSINESS PLAN = IMPLEMENTATION PLAN

If we assume that the idea and the configuration details of the idea might change significantly, we also need to ask ourselves if the implementation can be planned. Up to this point, it was the business plan that performed this task. The key benefit of a business plan is that it forces us early on to think through the implementation of an idea with a sufficient level of detail and put it down on paper. But we can't assume that the implementation will go according to plan. That is why the term "plan" is misleading.

FALSE ASSUMPTION 4:
ANALYZING AND PLANNING = RISK MINIMIZATION

The business plan represents the assumption that if we take enough time, analyze with enough precision, and plan a project right down to the nth detail, we can minimize the risk of failure. But how can we minimize risk through analysis and planning if the implementation often deviates extensively from the analysis and the plan? We should therefore not look for a better plan, but rather, find the route to a successfully implemented idea.[13] For this, we need a navigational tool – like the Lean Progress Model in this book.

On the facing page, you can see how investors feel when they're shown an overly optimistic growth curve, such as those produced on the basis of a traditional business plan. The curves resemble a hockey stick in shape, with a sharp bend depicting sudden and often inexplicable growth. Without any proof of actual customer demand, we can't trust these curves.

WHICH OF
THE THREE IDEAS
WOULD YOU
INVEST IN

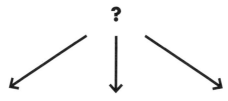

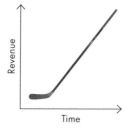

Fictional and overly optimistic financial plans – an investor's dilemma

TRADITIONAL RISK MINIMIZATION:
THROUGH REVOLUTION

The traditional approach assumes that the more we analyze, reflect and pre-plan from the outset, the more successful the innovation will be on the market. Once the idea has been selected and planned, we have to systematically implement it. We put all our eggs in one basket and hope that at the end of the process, the customers will also recognize the value added that we've planned for. Through sheer willpower, the innovation is to be introduced to the world and the market as a revolution.

A NEW SPIN ON RISK
MINIMIZATION

LEAN RISK MINIMIZATION:
THROUGH EVOLUTION

The Lean approach to risk is completely different. According to this approach, we need to be aware that many facets of the idea will change. We embark on the exploration and learning process with an open mind to find out which direction to follow in terms of developing the idea to ensure market viability. We go through small learning cycles to check over and over whether we're still on the right path or whether we need to change direction. Plus, as an established business, we don't just enter a single idea into the race, we also track several ideas simultaneously and let them compete against each other or against failure. Through iterative modeling and natural selection, the innovation is to be introduced to the world and the market as an evolution.

REVOLUTIONARY RISK MINIMIZATION

EVOLUTIONARY RISK MINIMIZATION

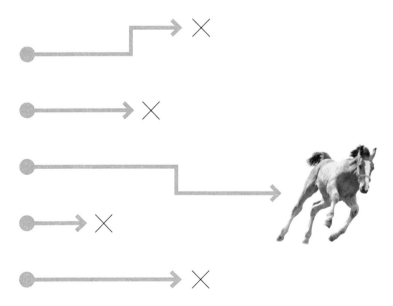

Risk minimization according to Lean happens through the evolutionary selection of projects

KEY TOOLS

L ean Innovation is supported by several tools and instruments. This chapter is a short and concise introduction to the key tools. They are being used worldwide and, in addition to the Lean Progress Model covered in this book, form an important foundation and complement to implement Lean Innovation appropriately and successfully.

OVERVIEW

BUSINESS MODEL CANVAS
Business Model Canvas is likely the best-known tool for identifying, describing and changing existing and new, innovative business models.[14] The visual and clearly structured design allows users to depict a business model on a single page and see the key components at a glance.

LEAN CANVAS
Lean Canvas is built on the graphical representation and concise structure of Business Model Canvas. However, some of the elements have been changed and optimized to better depict and change innovation ideas.[15]

INTERVIEWS AND OBSERVATION

Early and in-depth interactions with potential users and customers via interviews and through observation play a key role in Lean Innovation. There are guidelines and templates to help conduct interviews, an important but also challenging task.

PROTOTYPING AND MINIMUM VIABLE PRODUCT

The timely development of concrete and effective versions of a solution form another important Lean Innovation mainstay. What is key here is making a conscious decision between a prototype and a so-called minimum viable product.

FURTHER USEFUL TOOLS AND MODELS
WITH NO DESCRIPTION

- Empathy map
- Personas/User profile
- Customer journey
- User narratives
- Job-to-be-done framework
- Value proposition canvas
- Postmortem analysis
- Agile development/scrum
- A/B testing
- Usability testing

B usiness Model Canvas displays how a business model is built and configured on a single page, on the basis of nine key building blocks.[16] The building blocks are positioned such that the right side shows external factors from the market perspective, and the left side shows internal factors, as seen by the organization.

CUSTOMER SEGMENTS

An organization reaches and serves one or several customer segments. Other segments should only be set up if at least one of the other eight business model building blocks is changed as a result: for example, segment A pays a set price, whereas segment B is billed based on use.

BUSINESS MODEL CANVAS

VALUE PROPOSITIONS

With the value proposition, the organization promises to solve a customer segment's specific problem and thus meet needs. The components of a value proposition might consist of topics such as "convenience" (Nespresso), "aesthetic" (Apple), "cost reduction" (tax consultant) or "performance" (vacuum cleaner).

CHANNELS

The configuration of the channels indicates how customers are made aware of our offering (communication channels), how we are selling the offering (sales channels) and how the offering reaches the customers, whether digitally or physically (distribution channels).

COMPANY →   ← CUSTOMER

KEY PARTNERS	KEY ACTIVITIES	VALUE PROPOSITIONS	CUSTOMER RELATIONSHIPS	CUSTOMER SEGMENTS
	KEY RESOURCES		CHANNELS	

COST STRUCTURE	REVENUE STREAMS

Business Model Canvas (according to Osterwalder and Pigneur, 2012)

CUSTOMER RELATIONSHIPS

If we've attracted customers, we want to build a relationship with them that is as long and as positive as possible. The nature of the relationship can differ depending on the business model: for example, it could be one-one-one (advice in a clothing store), automated (Amazon recommendation algorithms) or self-serve (candy bar dispenser).

REVENUE STREAMS

The field of revenue streams describes the revenue model, so the way in which revenue is generated: for example, through the sales of physical goods (clothing store), the temporary rental of goods (car rentals), pay-per-use fees (phone usage based on number of minutes) or through membership dues (fitness center).

KEY RESOURCES AND KEY ACTIVITIES

Depending on the configuration of the previously listed building blocks in the business model, other types of key resources and activities might be needed to run the business model: for example, a production facility (resource) and quality management (activity) or software coding (resource) and software development (activity).

KEY PARTNERS

In certain cases, we don't want to do it all ourselves and work with key partners who will significantly boost the success of our business model. Here, you don't need to list every single supplier, just the key partners (for example, "machine manufacturers" for Nespresso).

COST STRUCTURE

Expenses related to resources and activities result in a corresponding cost structure. Here, too, only the key cost categories need to be listed.

Ideally, the Canvas is printed out as a poster and affixed to the wall. That way, you can stand in front of it and dynamically and creatively develop and improve new business models. What is important here, too, is that you never write directly on the Canvas, but rather, jot down each element of the configuration on a post-it note. This allows you to remain flexible and constantly go back to optimizing the business model, in addition to being forced to be concise in your modifications.

L ean Canvas represents a modification to Business Model Canvas.[17] The idea behind it was to replace individual building blocks of the business model with others, so that the innovation idea can be better represented in terms of content, and so that it can be tested and changed with the help of Lean Innovation methods. The business model building blocks not included in Lean Canvas are "Customer Relationships," "Key Resources," "Key Activities" and "Key Partners." Furthermore, "Value Proposition" has been supplemented with the word "Unique," so that we strive to clearly differentiate ourselves from our competitors. The newly integrated elements are explained and substantiated below.

LEAN CANVAS

PROBLEM
In this building block, a maximum of three of the most important problems that will be solved by an innovation project for the customer segment are to be listed. The next chapter will explain in more detail why innovations have to solve problems and which problems are of interest.

EXISTING ALTERNATIVES
This is where you note the currently available solutions. This is of utmost importance, as we need to be aware from the outset how potential customers approach problems today. This is the only way we can assess whether our new solution will really solve the problems in a manner that is markedly better, such that it results in real added value and we even have a chance at success. You also have to realize that the previous solutions and competitors are not always obvious. For example, the biggest competition for collaboration software is not necessarily another collaboration software, but rather, other forms of communication, such as e-mail or conversations.

PROBLEM	SOLUTION	UNIQUE VALUE PROPOSITION	UNFAIR ADVANTAGE	CUSTOMER SEGMENTS
	KEY METRICS		CHANNELS	
Existing Alternatives		High-Level Concept		Early Adopters
COST STRUCTURE		REVENUE STREAMS		

Lean Canvas (according to Maurya, 2012)

SOLUTION

This building block is where the three (maximum) most important solutions are noted. It might make sense here to not note the
solutions from the outset. First, we have to find the truly relevant
problems. The greater the changes to the problems, the more
closely the solutions need to adapt to these changes. If we wait
until later in the process to note the solutions, we can remain
more flexible. There's generally a risk that we already have set
solutions in our head at the beginning, and we try to define the
problems for these solutions instead of the other way around.

HIGH-LEVEL CONCEPT

The high-level concept condenses the innovation idea to a sentence that is as short and concise as possible, and that draws a
comparison with a familiar concept or idea. For example, "Flickr
for Videos" (YouTube) or "Facebook for businesses" (LinkedIn).
The high-level concept summarizes the idea, making it easier
to explain and disseminate. Because of its comparative nature,
listeners readily form an idea in their head of something they're
familiar with.[18]

EARLY ADOPTERS

The customer segment building blocks in Lean Canvas also allow
you to define the early prototype adopters. Which subsegment
might be most interested from the get-go? You should focus your
interaction and acquisition efforts on this target group first, as
they might help you achieve profitability most quickly.

UNFAIR ADVANTAGE

If applicable, this building block can be used to list actual unfair advantages. As soon as an innovation idea has been proven successful, there's a risk that copycats and competitors will enter the market. The bigger your competitive advantages are, or the harder they are to copy, the more challenging it will be for others to keep up. Good examples for this are hard-to-copy algorithms, patents, a unique customer base, or the community on a platform.

KEY METRICS

The key metrics building block is for listing the key metrics you're currently using to measure the success of your innovation project or of the underlying business model. In addition to the market's general strength of demand, which is detailed in the second part under the term "traction," we can measure sales funnel metrics, such as: 1. Potential customers, 2. Stakeholders, 3. Activated users 4. Paying customers, 5. Customers who recommend you.

Lean Canvas is a dynamic tool. This means that the contents will change constantly and only describe the current level of knowledge as a snapshot in the exploration and learning process according to Lean Innovation.

E xplorative interviews are a key instrument for interacting with and learning from potential customers and users. At first, it takes a bit of resolve to leave your desk and get out there to talk with people. But we can learn so much in a very short time. Even if interviews seem time-consuming at first glance, from a Lean approach perspective, they make a lot of sense: We can expect to save ten hours of development time for every hour invested in an interview.[19]

INTERVIEWS AND OBSERVATION

Conducting lean interviews according to Lean Innovation processes isn't very easy and needs some practice. The templates on the next few pages are a good support tool. You can download this and other tools from www.leaninnovationguide.com The first questionnaire is general in nature and can be used in every phase of the process. The two other questionnaires distinguish between problem and solution interviews. For every product, you first have to identify which problems the innovation project should solve. The solution isn't discussed at the beginning. There's always the risk of wanting to convince interview partners about our ideas for a solution, rather than trying to understand their problems. Don't fall into this trap! It's about learning, not selling. That's why we need to, above all else, listen to our potential clients and better understand what their world looks like, and how we can possibly support them with a better solution.

Another way to research user behavior is through observation. Observing potential customers solving problems in natural situations can provide important additional insights.

General interview template (adapted from Alvarez, 2014)

INFORMATION ON THE INTERVIEW Name, place and time, contact info, role, demographics, etc.

GENERAL QUESTIONS

1. Please explain how you currently resolve/deal with ....

2. Are there certain tools, products, apps, tricks or do you get help to do/resolve ....?

3. Who is involved in decisions in this field, and in what way?

4. Can you tell me how you last dealt with/resolved ....?

5. Can you please tell me more about the positive and negative experiences you had with this process?

6. If you were able to magically come up with a dream solution, what would it be?
   Note: It doesn't have to be realistic. Wish away, the sky's the limit!

7. Are there any topics in the field of .... that I should ask you about?
   Or what other key aspects can you expand on?

Other people or interview partners?

Would you like to receive updates? Can we contact you?

Thank you for your support!

Questionnaire for problem interviews (adapted from Maurya, 2012)

INFORMATION ON THE INTERVIEW Name, place and time, contact info, role, demographics, etc.

PROBLEM 1

How do you currently solve this problem?

Assessment of the problem (Intensity, frequency, overall relevance)

PROBLEM 2

How do you currently solve this problem?

Assessment of the problem (Intensity, frequency, overall relevance)

PROBLEM 3

How do you currently solve this problem?

Assessment of the problem (Intensity, frequency, overall relevance)

ADDITIONAL PROBLEMS NOT YET IDENTIFIED

Other people or interview partners?

Would you like to receive updates? Can we contact you?

Thank you for your support!

Questionnaire for solution interviews (adapted from Maurya, 2012)

INFORMATION ON THE INTERVIEW Name, place and time, contact info, role, demographics, etc.

SOLUTION 1

How would this solution be a better or worse solution to the problem?

Assessment of the solution (Enthusiasm, advantages, disadvantages, added value)

SOLUTION 2

How would this solution be a better or worse solution to the problem?

Assessment of the solution (Enthusiasm, advantages, disadvantages, added value)

SOLUTION 3

How would this solution be a better or worse solution to the problem?

Assessment of the solution (Enthusiasm, advantages, disadvantages, added value)

ADDITIONAL SOLUTIONS

TESTING THE PRICE "The price will be ...."
Reaction

Other people or interview partners?

Would you like to receive updates? Can we contact you?

Thank you for your support!

N ot until the relevant problems have been determined can potential customers be told about or shown the solutions. Interviews are the best and most lean way to interact with customers. However, if we only explain our ideas for solutions verbally, customers might have difficulties imagining them. That's why, later in the process, solutions are to be presented as a tangible prototype. This way, the reaction of potential customers will be more concrete and real. A prototype can test the aesthetic, technological and functional aspects, as well as the customers' acceptance. The exploration and learning process according to Lean Innovation is always in the foreground during this process. As soon as solutions take shape, the risk of waste and unnecessary development steps grows. We always have to ask ourselves: What do we need to learn next? And what are the minimum resources we do this with?

PROTOTYPING / MVP

The minimum viable product (MVP) represents a special type of prototype. This concept, developed in 2001, was adopted and promoted by the Lean Startup movement.[20] Opinions as to which early solution versions correspond to an MVP and which do not differ greatly. An MVP is supposed to speed up the learning process and test the key users of a solution. The value should actually be experienced and monetizable. MVPs do not consist of websites that raise awareness of a future offer, or clickable but non-functioning software prototypes. An MVP must deliver the key functionalities in a manner that is reliable, easy-to-use and emotionally and aesthetically pleasing. In the best-case scenario, customers should have to pay for its use from the outset. After all, if the key functionality can't be monetized, the business won't be viable.

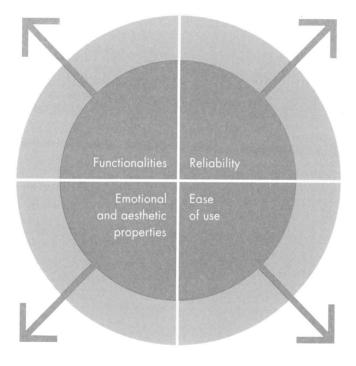

Four factors that an MVP takes into consideration and has to continuously improve

THE LEAN
PROGRESS
MODEL

A META MODEL FOR LEAN INNOVATION

The Lean Progress Model serves as a meta model for the high-level and transparent management of startup and innovation projects. It's only with this model that you can really successfully use the Lean approach and master the associated challenges. The three key advantages of the model are discussed on the next few pages.

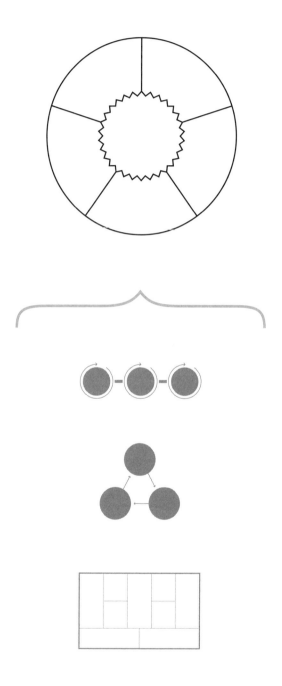

The Lean Progress Model as a meta model for the Lean Innovation process

1. MAXIMUM GUIDANCE

Without a business plan, there needs to be another transparent way to guide us and give us a sense as to where we currently find ourselves in the open exploration and learning process. The guidance should be as simple as possible. That's why the model only shows the six most important success factors of a startup or innovation project.

2. MAXIMUM FOCUS

In open innovation processes, we are confronted by countless design possibilities. Over and over again, we're spoiled for choice, and it can be so easy to lose ourselves. This is why it's so important that we maintain our focus and prioritize the learning steps based on the risks. The model, with its one guiding question and twelve sub-questions per success factor, helps us properly prioritize and maintain maximum focus while following a forward-looking approach to learning.

3. MAXIMUM SPEED

Many startup and innovation projects are much too slow from a learning process perspective. Insufficient speed represents one of the main sources of waste. The sooner we identify the route to success, the less we invest in going the wrong direction. Thanks to the color-coding in the model, we can identify the current status at a glance and are motivated to retest and optimize the open points as quickly as possible.

T he Lean Progress Model shows the six key success factors
of startup and innovation projects at a glance: (1) Problem,
(2) solution, (3) viability, (4) potential, (5) scalability and (6) traction.
The sixth factor, traction, measures the hopefully ever-increasing
proof of user and potential customer demand. We can directly
influence the factors in the outer circle of the model and config-
ure them accordingly, whereas the "traction" factor serves as an
indicator of the market.

MAXIMUM GUIDANCE: SIX SUCCESS FACTORS

The Lean Progress Model helps you maintain a high-level overview of the project, so at the highest level of abstraction. This is
very valuable both for collaborating in the project team and for
communicating with various internal and external stakeholder
groups, like top management or investors. The model thus provides maximum guidance, so that Lean Innovation can be successfully implemented.

THE LEAN PROGRESS MODEL

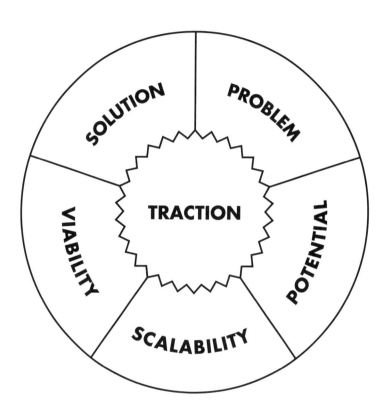

The six success factors of startup and innovation projects

Within the six success factors, a guiding question and several lower-level questions need to be answered. These guiding questions help you better navigate through the exploratory learning process, to focus on the questions that are currently most important in the process progress, and lastly, to really experience the Lean Innovation approach.

MAXIMUM FOCUS: PRIORITIZED GUIDING QUESTIONS

The open-ended questions guide us through the process according to Lean philosophy: First, we want to find out if it's even worth solving the problem. The new solution has to be better than alternative solutions. The potential has to be large and interesting enough, or be appropriate for the investment-risk relationship. The business and its business model must be viable. This means it has to be possible to profitably produce, offer and market the product. Naturally, one prerequisite is technical feasibility. Ideally, the startup or innovation project is scalable, ensuring quick and efficient growth. Traction as an indicator is at the center of the model and answers the question of whether potential customers on the market will react positively enough to our solution through increased use and purchases.

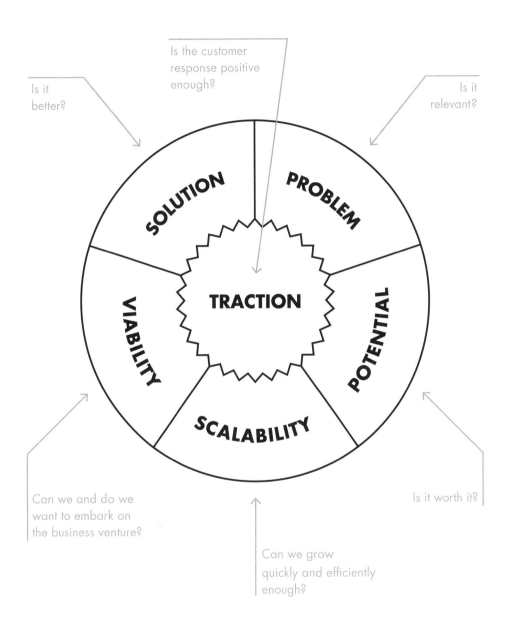

The key guiding questions for startup and innovation projects

I n order to identify as quickly as possible where the learning process and the assessment progress currently stand, the model uses the tried and true color coding of the traffic light system.

The colors let you see immediately where the startup or innovation project is in the process and which fields need to be optimized and tested as quickly as possible. For example, if the "problem" and "potential" fields are green, as shown in the image on the facing page, the "solution" field is red, and the "viability" field is assessed as yellow, we need to quickly test the solution field further and, if possible, optimize it. After ten to twelve weeks at most, it should be clear if an applicable problem can be solved with an approach that is notably better. This corresponds to the first "problem-solution fit" phase in the Lean Innovation process.

MAXIMUM SPEED: COLOR CODING

Color coding indicates where we need to quickly explore and learn more. It thus doesn't just contribute to high speed, but also helps—as do the guiding questions—us focus, so that whatever is next in importance or has the highest risk is always tested and optimized.

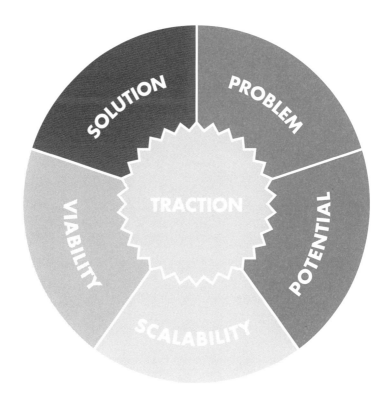

RED = negative assessment
GREEN = positive assessment
YELLOW = unclear assessment
COLORLESS = not yet tested

The traffic light colors show the process progress and motivate you
to test and optimize as quickly as possible.

SUCCESS FACTOR 1
IS IT RELEVANT?

F irst, we'll look at the success factor "problem" in the model. After all, an innovation can only be successful if it solves a problem that hasn't yet been solved (this is rare), that hasn't yet been solved satisfactorily enough, or if the solution to this problem can be fundamentally improved.

A problem is only good if it's relevant to the potential customer. If customers don't see the problem as such or if the problem isn't important enough, they will never be interested in a new solution, even if we solve the problem in a much better way. The opposite also holds true: if we come across a relevant problem, potential customers are generally very open to new solutions.

WHAT IS A GOOD PROBLEM?

The more important the problem is from the customer perspective and the more actively potential customers have been searching for a solution, the bigger the chances that an innovation will be successful. The problem-applicability pyramid shown on the facing page is a valuable tool for estimating the importance of a problem. The higher potential customers are categorized on the pyramid, the bigger the chances for the innovation's success.

The intensity and frequency of the problem are also to be factored in as part of the assessment: The longer, more frequently and extensively a problem occurs, the sooner it needs to be solved and the longer, more frequently and extensively the solution will be used. For example, we travel from home to other locations and back almost daily. It comes as no surprise that many projects try to address this attractive problem with innovations and traffic solutions.

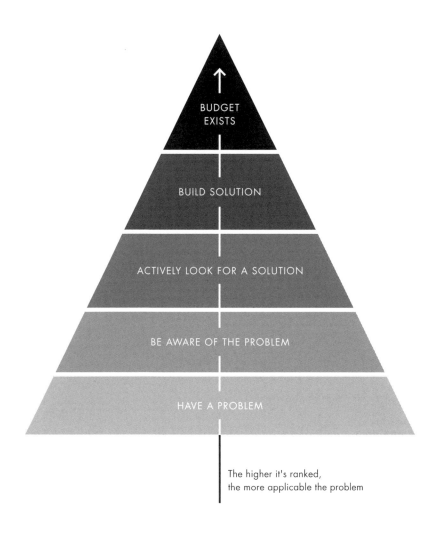

The problem-applicability pyramid (according to Blank et al., 2013)

I t's often more difficult for us to identify a relevant problem than to develop a good solution to a problem that has already been defined. We don't always solve the right problem from the outset. We often have to find out first which problems in a certain field or problem space are really worth solving.

ARE WE SOLVING
THE RIGHT PROBLEM?

But how do we find the right problems? On the one hand, by describing their current situation, customers will give us clues indicating attractive problems. On the other hand, we can also conduct an extensive and analytical exploration of the problem space and if necessary, redefine it. The "problem reframing technique" is a good approach to follow here.[21] The diagram shows how we use the technique to get from the slow elevator problem to the problem of tedious waiting and from there, to totally new approaches to a solution.

A similar direction is followed by the "jobs-to-be-done approach"[22], which tries to find the job underlying supposed and obvious problems or needs, and that can be resolved by a solution. This also leads to different approaches to a solution. To illustrate this approach, we often see the example of the milkshake, a beverage that doesn't necessarily just satiate the commuter, but also "sweetens" the long commute so typical to North American life.

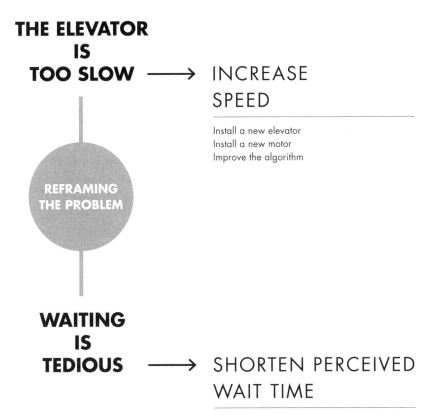

The problem reframing technique (Wedell-Wedellsborg, 2017)

S ome people generally object to the term "problem" in the field of innovation or management. Some argue that it's more of a pessimistic term and should be replaced with the term "challenge." Others point out that potential customers don't have problems, they have needs that have to be met. And then there are others who talk about "pains" that need to be relieved.

WHY THE TERM "PROBLEM"?

In my opinion, we should agree on the term "problem" in the field of startups and innovations, but use it and interpret it in a neutral sense, as it is not negative per se. There are many reasons for choosing the term "problem":

1. Designating a situation as a problem makes us perceive it as more important and applicable than when we talk about a challenge or a need.

2. Every challenge and need can also be translated as a problem. If we do that, it makes it clearer which solution could be valuable for the problem.

3. If we use the term "need," we often end up in discussions as to whether the needs have to exist beforehand or whether we can also create them. There is a risk that we will look for a need for our solution, rather than the other way around. In addition, a need demands that customers' thoughts are already turned towards a solution, which limits the solution space.

4. The term "pain" is often used as a synonym for problems. However, this is incorrect, as problems can result in "pain," which can have varying intensities, depending on the problem. It's about indirect side-effects and not the core that needs to be solved.

PROBLEM
IT TAKES TOO LONG TO GET
FROM A TO B

DESIRE
I WANT A
FASTER HORSE

CHALLENGE
HOW DO I FIND
THE FASTEST HORSE
IN THE REGION?

PAIN
IT IS TIRING
TO SIT ON A HORSE
FOR A LONG TIME

The word "problem" as the best benchmark for innovations

O ver and over again, the question of whether we can create needs arises. After all, there are solutions whose success we would never have imagined and that satisfy a need that no potential customer knew they had. Take, for example, Apple's iPhone, or the Japanese toy "Tamagotchi," a handheld digital egg that needs to be raised like a pet or a child. Both solutions made needs obvious that most customers never knew they had: the desire for a smartphone or the need to feed a digital animal and take care of it.

These very concrete needs are created in a certain way. But behind every need is a more abstract need that was generally already there. If we climb down this ladder of needs, the needs become increasingly abstract, and at some point, we end up at basic needs, according to Maslow.[23] The more abstract or basic the needs are, the more difficult they are to create.

SOLVING PROBLEMS VS. CREATING DESIRE

Around the turn of the millennium, ever more customers were demanding mobile phones, MP3 players and digital assistants. Some people wanted a single device that united all this functionality. The iPhone didn't create that need until it reached the sixth level of abstraction, as depicted in the diagram on the facing page. In response to the question of what they wanted, customers didn't describe an iPhone, but they likely mentioned the problem of ever-increasing numbers of mobile devices, which would have been interpreted as the iPhone being the solution.

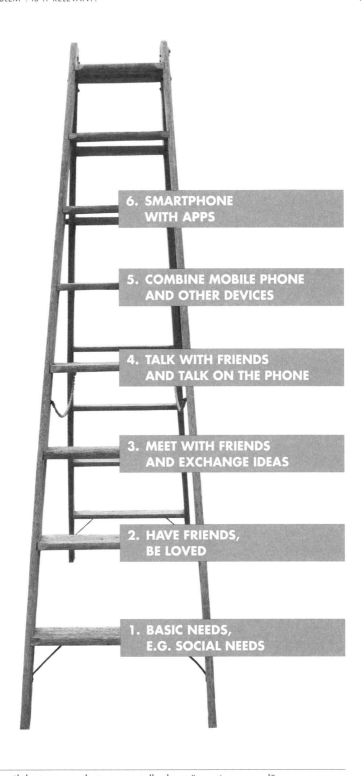

It's not until the top rung that we can talk about "creating a need"

1. **WHY SHOULD MARK USE EMAIL?**

LOOKING AT THE FEELINGS BEHIND THE PROBLEM

SO HE CAN SEND AND RECEIVE MESSAGES.

2. **WHY SHOULD MARK DO THAT?**

TO QUICKLY EXCHANGE IDEAS.

With the 5 whys technique, we ask about the reason five times, so we can get to the root cause of the problem. The technique was developed by Toyota and was originally used for quality management purposes. But it also makes it possible to get to the feelings underlying the supposedly rational problems.[24] Once we know the emotional level of the problems, we can develop solutions that address these feelings, making them more applicable.

Identifying the feelings underlying the supposedly rational problem using the 5 whys
(according to Eyal, 2014)

M any startup and innovation projects start with an idea for a solution. The people involved start by focusing on the solution and their ingenuity, instead of on which problem should be solved and how the solution produces benefits from the perspective of the problem. However, without a relevant problem or one that isn't solved well enough, no real added value will result.

FROM HAVING IDEAS
TO SOLVING PROBLEMS

It would therefore make sense for businesses, at least those in the field of innovation, to move away from an idea-generating culture to a problem-solving culture. Solutions are an ego thing and beg to be defended and sold internally. They didn't come up with the saying "kill your darlings" for nothing. If we focus more on the customers' and users' problems, we act with more empathy than if we think mostly in terms of solutions. Problems are to be sought with the customer, independently of us, and they form the basis for true added value.

A culture of problem-solving can be promoted through various measures. Here are a few ideas to inspire:
– When a solution is suggested, always ask what problem is being solved.
– Find out the underlying emotional reasons using the 5 whys (see page 94 et seq.).
– Focus the innovation projects on one to three key problems. The problems to be solved should be omnipresent (for example, posted in the conference room).
– Rename sellers and innovators "problem-solvers" or something similar.

MAIN QUESTION
SUCCESS FACTOR
"PROBLEM"

PROBLE

RE

ENOUG

IS THE

M

LEVANT

H ?

SUB-QUESTIONS
SUCCESS FACTOR
"PROBLEM"

1 HOW RELEVANT IS THE PROBLEM FOR POTENTIAL CUSTOMERS?

2 ARE POTENTIAL CUSTOMERS AWARE OF THE PROBLEM?

5 HOW MUCH MORE OF A POSITIVE IMPACT WOULD A BETTER SOLUTION HAVE?

6 HAVE POTENTIAL CUSTOMERS ALREADY LOOKED FOR A SOLUTION?

9 ARE POTENTIAL CUSTOMERS ENTHUSIASTIC WITH RESPECT TO A NEW SOLUTION?

10 WHICH KEY PROBLEM IS THE FOCUS AND WHAT ARE THE LOWER-LEVEL PROBLEMS?

3 HOW OFTEN AND FOR HOW LONG HAS THE PROBLEM BEEN HAPPENING?

4 HOW MUCH OF A PAIN AND HOW EXTREME IS THE PROBLEM?

7 HAVE POTENTIAL CUSTOMERS ALREADY TRIED TO SOLVE THE PROBLEM THEMSELVES?

8 ARE POTENTIAL CUSTOMERS ENTHUSIASTIC WITH RESPECT TO THE PROBLEM?

11 WHICH ASPECTS OF THE PROBLEM DO WE STILL NEED TO BETTER UNDERSTAND?

12 ARE THERE RELATED PROBLEMS THAT WE STILL NEED TO TAKE INTO CONSIDERATION?

RED

YELLOW

GREEN

NEGATIVE RESPONSE TO THE SOLUTION
THE PROBLEM ISN'T A PROBLEM, OR IT'S NOT IMPORTANT ENOUGH

The potential customers are pretty happy with the current situation as it is. That's why they have no wish to help in further development or to find out about new solutions.

UNCLEAR RESPONSE TO THE SOLUTION
THE POTENTIAL CUSTOMERS HAVE A PROBLEM OR ARE MODERATELY SATISFIED WITH THE CURRENT SITUATION

Nevertheless, they don't know which problem needs to be solved. We might be on the trail of something interesting, but it's not clear, what it is. Potential customers are open to new solutions, but have neither actively looked for them nor developed their own solution. They're open to the matter and to new solutions, but don't react enthusiastically.

POSITIVE RESPONSE TO THE SOLUTION
POTENTIAL CUSTOMERS REACT VERY ENTHUSIASTICALLY TO THE PROSPECT OF A NEW, BETTER SOLUTION TO A VERY CLEAR PROBLEM.

They readily provide information about the problem and want to know more about the solution and stay informed. Some of the potential customers want to help us better understand and develop a better solution. Some have already tried to develop a workaround.

SUCCESS FACTOR 2
IS THE SOLUTION BETTER?

T he more valuable the solution seems to be to the customer, the greater the chance of success. The perceived value depends on how relevant the problem to be solved is. The solution for an unimportant problem might be really good, but the added value is still low. For example, when we're riding a bicycle, we have to (mostly) take our hand off the handlebars to ring the bell. This is a relatively insignificant problem, so an innovative bell would only deliver limited added value. Compare this to an innovative tire that will no longer rupture, thus solving the significant problem of dealing with a flat and the tediousness of changing the tire. So, a good solution needs, first and foremost, a relevant problem.

WHAT IS A GOOD SOLUTION?

Secondly, the new solution has to differentiate itself positively and distinctively from the existing solution. The better the current solutions for a problem are, the harder it will be to get an even better solution on the market and to convince customers to switch. The greater the positive difference to the existing solutions, the bigger the experienced added value from a customer perspective.

Finally, the added value is lessened through so-called switching costs. For example, this refers to the effort of learning a new solution, or the loss of the data input in the previous solution.

SOLUTION VALUE

$$SV =$$

PROBLEM-RELEVANCE   INTENSITY   FREQUENCY   BUDGET

$$pr(i \times f \times b)$$

$$+ pav - sc$$

POTENTIAL ADDED VALUE
AS COMPARED TO
THE ALTERNATE SOLUTION

SWITCHING COSTS

S tartup and innovation teams want their solutions to improve or simplify people's lives. It's worth understanding as well as possible why and how added value comes to be as a result. Because if we understand how we can improve or simplify our customer's life, we can further increase the resulting value.

WHAT TYPE OF ADDED VALUE DOES THE SOLUTION DELIVER?

Being aware of a few general value types will aid in our understanding. In a Harvard Business Review study, thirty such different types of value could be identified,[25] divided into four categories by the authors: (1) functional, (2) emotional, (3) life-changing and (4) concerning social impact. In most cases, solutions provide a combination of value types. The overview of the value types helps us, on the one hand, further clarify very general customer responses—such as "convenient"—with several value types.[26] For example, the added value of a "convenient" bank could be rewritten and prioritized using elements such as "saves time," "avoids hassles," "simplifies," and "reduces effort." On the other hand, the overview of the value elements can be used as a design and creativity tool in the development of innovation solutions.

SOCIAL IMPACT

LIFE-CHANGING

EMOTIONAL

FUNCTIONAL

Potential value types for private users (according to Almquist et al., 2016)

There's a difference between creating added value for private end users or companies. In the case of corporate customers, their financial success is front and center. We can achieve this for them through higher customer satisfaction and thus potentially higher margins, through cost reduction or a revenue increase. Naturally, individual employees aren't working for the financial success of the company; they'd also like to be more successful on a personal level and be appreciated accordingly.

ADDED VALUE FOR CORPORATE CUSTOMERS

In the private sphere, financial aspects are of secondary importance. We'd much rather be happy, feel good, and be socially valued. However, the current zeitgeist indicates an increased merging of private and professional needs, especially through the very purpose-driven Generations Y and Z. Over the long term, the financial success of a company will remain front and center, but a company's purpose and having a positive societal impact is becoming ever more important.

In another Harvard Business Review study, authors identified forty types of value in the field of corporate customers (Business-to-Business). They categorized them as follows:[27]

– Table stakes (barrier to entry)
– Functional stakes (economic efficiency and performance)
– Ease of doing business (productivity, operation, access, provider-customer relationships, strategies)
– Individual value (personal and career)
– Inspirational value

In the case of corporate customers, the table stakes, functional stakes and ease of doing business take center stage. These value fields form the foundation for buyers or project managers. Incidentally, competition also occurs mostly at this level. The elements of value are therefore fought over, making them interchangeable. How the individual people involved feel and behave towards corporate customers is no less important. In the field of corporate business, when we also venture into the level of individual and inspirational values, a hard-to-replicate differentiation and an emotional connection can result.

As with the types of value in the private sphere, the forty elements of value can be used as a guideline and as a design and creativity tool for startup and innovation projects.

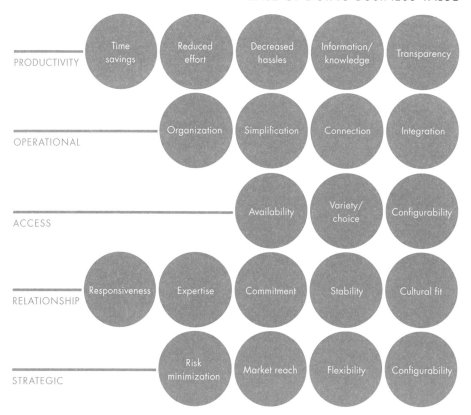

TABLE STAKES

EASE OF DOING BUSINESS VALUE

PRODUCTIVITY

- Time savings
- Reduced effort
- Decreased hassles
- Information/knowledge
- Transparency

OPERATIONAL

- Organization
- Simplification
- Connection
- Integration

ACCESS

- Availability
- Variety/choice
- Configurability

RELATIONSHIP

- Responsiveness
- Expertise
- Commitment
- Stability
- Cultural fit

STRATEGIC

- Risk minimization
- Market reach
- Flexibility
- Configurability

FUNCTIONAL VALUE

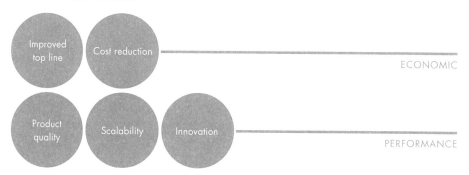

INDIVIDUAL VALUE

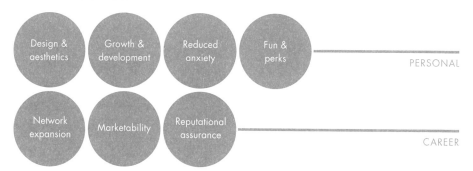

INSPIRATIONAL VALUE

Potential types of value for business users (according to Almquist et al., 2018)

A s already mentioned, the added value of new offerings is not only produced in isolation through a good solution. Potential clients always assess the added value on the basis of previous solutions. On the one hand, the improvement has to be distinct and easily identifiable, and on the other hand, it has to be worthwhile to switch from the previous to the new solution. This gives rise to switching costs.

VALUE ADDED FOR ALTERNATIVE SOLUTIONS

As the provider of a new solution, we want to understand which factors drive a customer to switch, and which factors prevent them from switching. Both the previous solutions and the new solution can facilitate or impede a switch. On the basis of these considerations, an analysis tool was created[28] that allows us to identify which factors of the new solution and which factors of the previous solution are more likely to encourage or impede a switch.

Supporting a solution switch: The four strengths diagram

Switching to a new solution is greatly facilitated by the simplicity of the solution and the switch. The easier it is for the users to accept a new solution, try it out and adapt their behavior, the more likely it is that the switch will take place. For example, what moves us to switch from a digital camera to a mobile phone camera? You always have your mobile phone on you, and you can delete new photos with a simple click.

SIMPLICITY FACILITATES A SWITCH

A behavioral scientist from Stanford University recognized this and lists simplicity, along with the necessary motivation and a trigger as the key prerequisite for behavioral change.[29] New solutions can be simplified to six levels: 1. time, 2. money, 3. effort, 4. mental effort, 5. social acceptance and 6. deviation from routine. In considering these fields, we should always ask ourselves: What complicates the behavior we wish to see for potential users and customers? And how can we design our products and services so that the desired behavior is as easy as possible?

The way in which simplicity drives behavior can be illustrated using social media content as an example.[30] The easier it is to generate content, the higher the number of users who develop their own content. While at first, it was just a few bloggers who published texts with a relative amount of effort, new services cropped up, like Facebook or Twitter, where content has to be short, making it easier to generate. With Pinterest, it's even easier to develop content, because all users have to do is select images and curate them by topic.

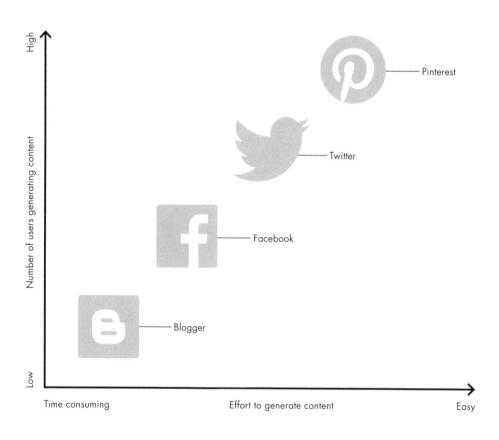

The easier it is to use, the more likely we are to change behavior (Eyal, 2014)

IS THE

SIGN

BETTER T

ALT

SOLUTION

SOLUTION

FICANTLY

HAN

ERNATIVE

S ?

SUB-QUESTIONS
SUCCESS FACTOR
"SOLUTION"

1 **HOW DO POTENTIAL CUSTOMERS SOLVE THE PROBLEM NOW?**

2 **WHY DID THEY CHOOSE THE CURRENT SOLUTION OR NO SOLUTION?**

5 **HOW ENTHUSIASTIC IS THE REACTION TO THE PROSPECT OF A NEW SOLUTION?**

6 **WHICH AREAS OF THE SOLUTION ARE VALUABLE AND WHICH NEED TO BE IMPROVED?**

9 **WHAT TYPE(S) OF ADDED VALUE DOES OUR SOLUTION CURRENTLY DELIVER?**

10 **WHICH FACTORS PROMOTE OR PREVENT THE SWITCH TO THE NEW SOLUTION?**

3 HAVE POTENTIAL CUSTOMERS ALREADY LOOKED FOR A NEW SOLUTION?

4 IF YES, WHAT TYPE OF SOLUTION DID THEY LOOK FOR?

7 WHICH MINIMUM KEY FUNCTION-ALITIES (MVP) ARE CUSTOMERS PREPARED TO PAY FOR?

8 HOW MUCH ARE POTENTIAL CUSTOMERS PREPARED TO PAY?

11 WHICH ASPECTS OF AN OPTIMIZED SOLUTION DO WE STILL NEED TO BETTER UNDERSTAND?

12 WHICH RELATED ASPECTS OF THE SOLUTION HAVE WE NOT YET THOUGHT OF?

RED

YELLOW

GREEN

NEGATIVE RESPONSE TO THE SOLUTION
POTENTIAL CUSTOMERS DO NOT SEE THE ADDED VALUE OF A NEW SOLUTION.

Either they're satisfied enough with existing solutions or the value we've proposed is lower than assumed, or our supposed advantage is in the wrong value field, or it is not recognized by the customer as such.

UNCLEAR RESPONSE TO THE SOLUTION
POTENTIAL CUSTOMERS RECOGNIZE THAT A NEW SOLUTION MIGHT DELIVER ADDED VALUE.

However, they don't yet fully understand how our new solution can provide them with added value. Potential customers are open to a new solution and generally interested, but they're not enthusiastic.

POSITIVE RESPONSE TO THE SOLUTION
POTENTIAL CUSTOMERS GENERALLY REACT ENTHUSIASTICALLY TO A NEW SOLUTION AND ESPECIALLY TO OUR SOLUTION.

They quickly recognize the added value and the benefits of our solution. They absolutely want to find out more about the solution and be informed in the future. Some of the potential customers want to actively help with further development.

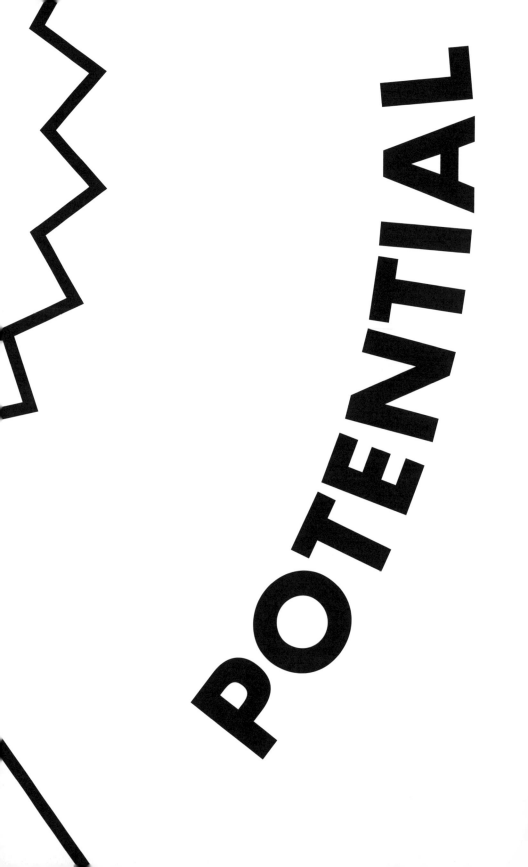

SUCCESS FACTOR 3
IS IT WORTH IT?

W e use the success factor "potential" to check whether it's even worth continuing a project in terms of the potential number of users and the potential revenue. Particularly when we compare several ideas and projects, potential is an important criterion for the targeted distribution of limited resources to the most attractive projects.

In the second phase of the Lean Innovation process, we find out if there is even a market for our new solution (product-market fit). The definition of the market or of the interested customer segment can change constantly throughout the process. The assessment of potential is to be constantly adapted accordingly. For example, if we determine that only a niche comes into question, and not a mass market, we have to once again clarify whether or not the size of the niche is of interest.

A BROAD OR NARROW MARKET DEFINITION?

If we're given the opportunity to convince an internal or external stakeholder of our innovation idea, we present the potential as attractively as possible. In this case, a top-down calculation makes sense. A very large market volume is compared to a very small and thus attainable market share that still appears very financially interesting: "We (just) have to achieve 1% of the market volume as our market share, which would lead to very high revenues and profits."

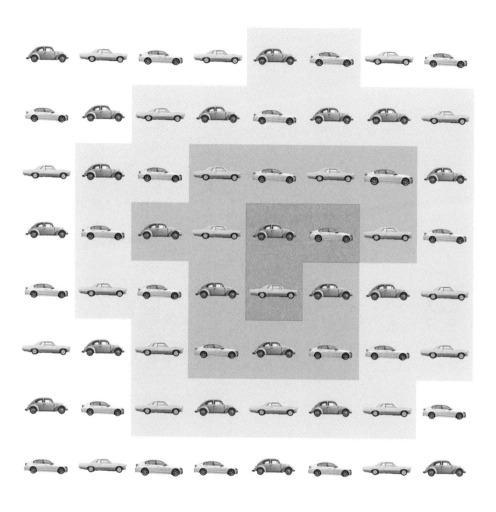

☐ Car owners
▨ Additional earnings important
▨ Car not used often
▨ Car publicly accessible

A realistic assessment of potential requires a market definition that is on the narrow side
(example: Private carsharing)

I f we're given the opportunity to convince an internal or external stakeholder of our innovation idea, we present the potential as attractively as possible. In this case, a top-down calculation makes sense. A very large market volume is compared to a very small and thus attainable market share that still appears very financially interesting: "We (just) have to achieve 1% of the market volume as our market share, which would lead to very high revenues and profits."

FROM A TOP-DOWN CALCULATION...

In evaluating the success factor "potential" in the Lean Progress Model, we're striving for a more realistic assessment. The following reasons speak against a top-down approach:[31]

1. It gives us a false sense of security.
2. It doesn't state how we'll acquire the "small" market share.
3. For startup and innovation projects, the market share is rarely the right indicator at the beginning.

For example, if we tackle the Chinese market, our focus shouldn't be on just having to reach 1% of the Chinese population, but rather, it should be on how the absolute number of approximately 14 million Chinese will find out about our solution, be interested in it, try it, and then, in the end, purchase it.

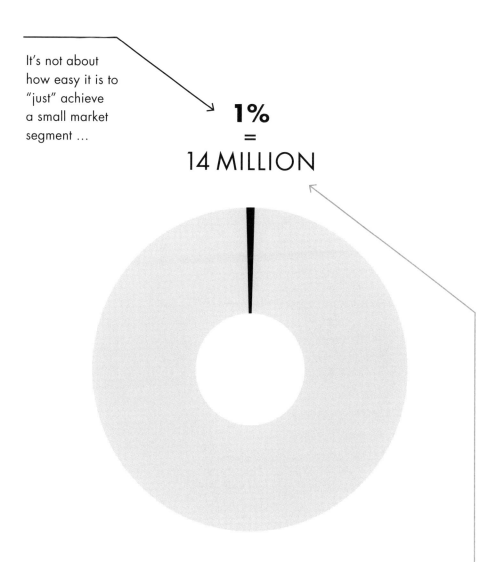

It's not about
how easy it is to
"just" achieve
a small market
segment …

1%
=
14 MILLION

… it's about how hard it
is to even get 14 million
potential customers to find
out about our solution,
to be interested in it, and
to even end up buying it.

A top-down calculation gives a false sense of security

T he bottom-up assessment of potential is done using a detailed calculation based on empirical variables such as a customer's cumulative revenues. This is how we obtain a much more realistic picture, o n the one hand, and on the other hand, we can continuously measure the relevant indicators and learn from the changes.

... TO A BOTTOM-UP-CALCULATION

For the bottom-up calculation, we're using Ash Maurya's[32] approach, starting with a future annual target revenue. In the example shown, we want to take in one million dollars in the third year. Now we estimate a customer's lifetime value. In the example, we're assuming a monthly revenue of 30 US dollars over two years. With this information, we can calculate two variables, which allow us to assess whether this potential can be achieved and maintained in the future. If we divide the target revenue by a customer's annual revenue, we get the number of active customers, which allows us to assess whether we can "manage" them efficiently enough with our business model. The example shows 2,778 active customers. When we divide the target revenue by the lifetime value, we get the number of new customers gained annually and who have to be "channeled" through our business model. Our example shows this to be 1,389 new customers annually. Here, too, we need to ask ourselves whether and how we can acquire these new customers efficiently enough. If the monthly revenues per customer increase or if their lifetime can be lengthened, the business model's so-called throughput will increase.

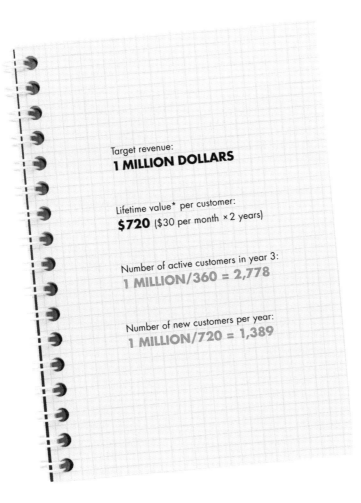

Target revenue:
1 MILLION DOLLARS

Lifetime value* per customer:
$720 ($30 per month × 2 years)

Number of active customers in year 3:
1 MILLION/360 = 2,778

Number of new customers per year:
1 MILLION/720 = 1,389

* We can also use the lifetime value to calculate
the monthly churn rate:
100%/24 months = 4.17%.

Conversely, we can use this rate to figure out
how many customers we need to acquire annually:
12 × 4.17% × 2,778 = 1,389

Bottom-up calculation of a startup or innovation project (according to Maurya, 2017)

T he number of customers is depicted over time. The number of theoretically achievable customers in the long term is determined using the top-down approach, whereas the number of customers achievable in the short- and medium-term is calculated from the bottom up. We can either derive the latter from the target revenue, as described on the previous pages, or we do our estimates and calculations using a realistic result that can be achieved through concrete acquisition and distribution channels.

BOTTOM-UP: NUMBER OF CUSTOMERS

The bottom-up calculation on the basis of concrete acquisition and distribution channels:

SOM SERVICEABLE OBTAINABLE MARKET
The number of existing or short-term obtainable customers that can be acquired with the help of existing or immediately implementable acquisition and distribution channels.
SAM SERVICEABLE AVAILABLE MARKET
The number of medium-term obtainable customers that can be acquired with the help of planned acquisition and distribution channels in the next three to five years.

The top-down calculation using an assessment of the theoretical market share:

TAM TOTAL ADDRESSABLE MARKET
The theoretical number of customers and the corresponding market share that we can reach in the long term.
PAM POTENTIALLY AVAILABLE MARKET
The theoretical market value shared by all competitors.

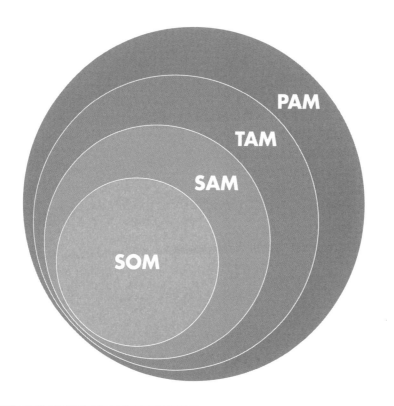

Time ⟶

SOM
Achievable market with the current means,
30 universities

        SAM
        Achievable market with the planned channels,
        200 universities

                TAM
                Addressable market,
                1,000 universities

                        PAM
                        Addressable market,
                        17,000 universities

Calculation of the number of customers over time (example: Product for universities)

T he ustomer lifetime value (CLV, CLTV, LCV or LTV) describes the revenue a customer achieves during their customer lifetime with a company. Because this number applies to the future and cannot be properly projected on the basis of empirical values, calculating it can be challenging. However, it is still worthwhile to use this value, because when compared to acquisition costs, it indicates what the available maximum available budget is to acquire a customer.

BOTTOM-UP: LIFETIME VALUE

As a rule of thumb, we often see that the lifetime value has to correspond to at least three times the acquisition costs in order to profitably acquire customers and be able to channel them through the business model:

Lifetime value ≥ 3 × acquisition costs

The calculation of lifetime value can be done in one of three ways: If we still have no customers, the only option we have is to estimate. If we have initial customers and churn, we can use the churn rate as the basis for our calculations. If we've had a long experience with customers, we can calculate the average lifetime using historic data.

REVENUE BY CUSTOMER BY MONTH × NUMBER OF MONTHS

NO CUSTOMERS YET
ESTIMATE NUMBERS

FIRST CUSTOMERS
AND CHURN
**1 / AVERAGE MONTHLY
CHURN RATE IN %**

LIFETIME KNOWN
**CURRENT
AVERAGE LIFETIME**

Calculating lifetime value depending on the development phase

C ustomer acquisition costs (CAC) include all financial and other directly attributable means that a company needs to invest in order to attract a new customer. This includes things like advertising, public relations, sales personnel, samples, or the costs of introducing customers to the new solution.

BOTTOM-UP:
ACQUISITION COSTS

If we subtract the customer acquisition costs per customer from the lifetime value, we can determine if acquisition expenses are reasonably balanced and from what point acquisition expenses are amortized (see image on facing page). We can also calculate what residual value remains to cover other costs. This calculation is key for investors because their resources should flow mainly into acquisition so that growth can be sped up in a cost-effective manner.

In conclusion, the value helps us estimate whether the number of customers to be acquired annually seems realistic based on the calculation on page 130, and what we can expect in terms of annual total acquisition expenses.

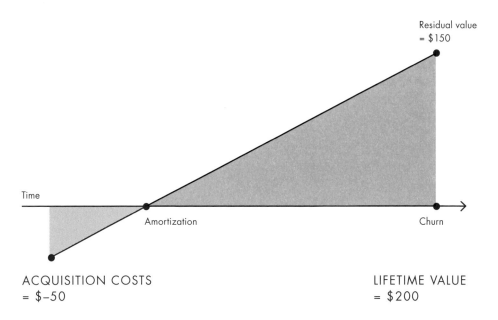

Residual value
= $150

Time

Amortization

Churn

ACQUISITION COSTS
= $–50

LIFETIME VALUE
= $200

Ratio of acquisition costs to lifetime value

E ven if a market is interesting from a financial perspective, it also needs to be assessed from a qualitative perspective. For example, the mobile payment market is extremely attractive from a financial viewpoint, but on the one hand, there are lots of competitors working on developing a solution in this sector, and on the other hand, global—and therefore active—corporations like Apple, Google or Samsung have nearly unrivaled market power with an exceptionally large existing user base. The financial potential in the mobile payment sector would thus be extremely high, but from a qualitative perspective, this potential is almost unattainable.

QUALITATIVE ANALYSIS: THE SECTOR

Porter's five competitive forces can be used to analyze market attractiveness.[33] As a slightly older analysis tool, the five competitive forces can be updated with regard to innovation projects:

Rivalry: Are there already lots of competitors on the market? How strong are these competitors?

Customers: Do the customers have a large selection of existing solutions and a correspondingly large negotiating power that will drop the price?

Suppliers: Are we highly dependent on our own suppliers, who could increase the costs of the innovation idea accordingly?

Potential competitors: Are there lots of competitors interested in an innovation in our sector and are any of them currently working on them, or planning to do so?

Substitute products: Which substitute products or future solutions could potential customers switch to?

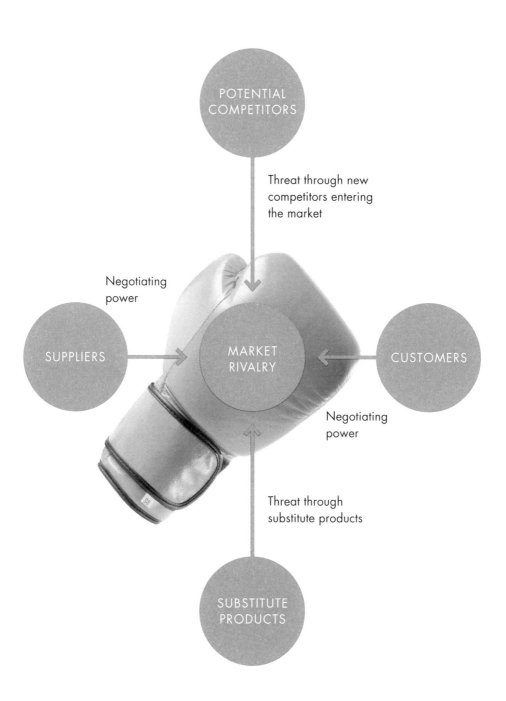

Qualitative analysis of the sector using the five forces analysis (adapted from Porter, 2008)

I n addition to a sector and competitor analysis, the macro environment, with its opportunities and hazards, needs to be taken into consideration. The macro environment can have a positive or negative impact on market attractiveness, and thus also on potential.

Take the taxi service Uber, for example. They decided on a very lucrative market. However, Uber found out that the legal situation for taxi services had changed for the worse. In many countries and cities, taxi drivers need a license, whereas Uber drivers can do without one and are considered independent businesses. This means that Uber doesn't have to make any social security contributions. This led to an extensive legal battle and was very costly for Uber, in addition to attracting negative publicity.

QUALITATIVE ANALYSIS: THE MACRO ENVIRONMENT

It's not that the factors making up the macro environment totally change the assessment of potential, but it's good to know early on which factors could negatively or positively change the assessment of the potential.

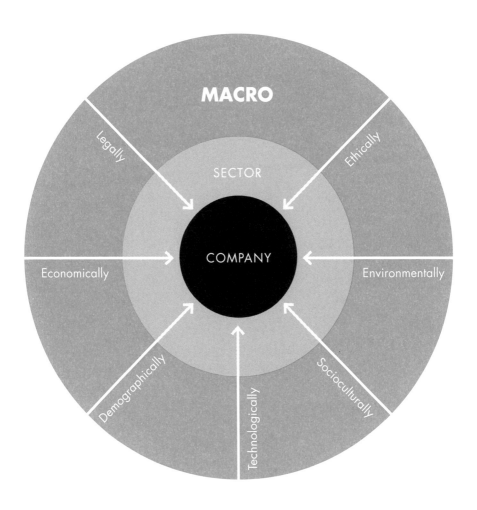

How and to what extent are we dependent on the macro environment?

WORT

PUR

THE ID

IS IT WORTH PURSUING THIS IDEA?

1 WHICH SECTOR
AND WHICH
MARKET DOES
THE IDEA
BELONG TO?

2 HOW MANY PEOPLE
CAN WE PROVIDE
ADDED VALUE TO?

5 WHAT IS THE
RATIO OF
LIFETIME VALUE
TO ACQUISITION
COSTS?

6 WHAT REVENUE
POTENTIAL CAN WE
ACHIEVE IN THE
SHORT- AND MEDIUM-
TERM?

9 WOULD THE IDEA
ALSO BE WORTH-
WHILE IF WE
WERE TO ONLY
ADDRESS THE
SMALLEST NICHE
MARKET?

10 HOW ATTRACTIVE
IS THE MARKET
WE'RE CURRENTLY
STRIVING FOR FROM
A QUALITATIVE
PERSPECTIVE?

3 HOW LARGE IS OUR LONG-TERM REVENUE POTENTIAL IN THIS MARKET?

4 HOW LARGE IS A CUSTOMER'S LIFETIME VALUE?

7 WHICH SMALLEST NICHE COULD STILL BE CONSIDERED FOR OUR IDEA?

8 HOW LARGE WOULD THE REVENUE POTENTIAL OF THE SMALLEST NICHE BE?

11 WHICH OPPOR-TUNITIES AND HAZARDS ARE CONNECTED WITH THE MARKET?

12 TO WHAT EXTENT DOES THE MACRO ENVIRONMENT AFFECT MARKET ATTRACTIVENESS?

RED

YELLOW

GREEN

NEGATIVE ASSESSMENT OF THE POTENTIAL
THE TARGETED MARKET AND THE SHORT- AND MEDIUM-TERM ACHIEVABLE CUSTOMER SEGMENTS ARE NOT INTERESTING ENOUGH.

This applies both in terms of quantity and quality. We have to either find another market or change the innovation project in such a way that the market can be assessed as more attractive.

UNCLEAR ASSESSMENT OF THE POTENTIAL
THE TARGETED MARKET AND THE SHORT- AND LONG-TERM ACHIEVABLE CUSTOMER SEGMENTS ARE NOT YET INTERESTING ENOUGH IN TERMS OF QUANTITY OR QUALITY.

It's currently not clear whether the overall potential can be assessed more as negative or more as positive. We will continue our analysis, but will have to reassess in the near future whether the investment of time and money is worthwhile in terms of potential.

POSITIVE ASSESSMENT OF THE POTENTIAL
THE TARGETED MARKET AND THE SHORT- AND MEDIUM-TERM ACHIEVABLE CUSTOMER SEGMENTS ARE INTERESTING BOTH IN TERMS OF QUANTITY AND QUALITY AND VERY PROMISING.

However, this assessment needs to be verified at regular intervals, as new insights or changed framework conditions could lead to a new assessment from both a financial and qualitative perspective. Either way, if we change customer segments, we have to reassess the potential.

SUCCESS FACTOR 4
CAN WE AND DO WE WANT TO?

VIABILITY

We use the success factor "viability" to look into whether the business is feasible and viable. The feasibility of a new, innovative product is rarely the problem,[34] except for very long-term oriented and completely new developments, where the technological feasibility is the primary focus. This applies to basic research in the field of medicine, for example, or to the search for totally new sources of energy. However, most innovations are usually technically doable. The key question is then whether the business model behind the product idea is viable. Viable means users are showing enough interest and are ready to pay for it accordingly, and that we can deliver the offering efficiently enough, and also want to, so that we end up with a profit.

THE BUSINESS MODEL AS A BENCHMARK FOR VIABILITY

Not just products and services have a business model, so do process innovations or offerings from non-profit organizations. Time and financial resources are invested into every idea, which then has to recover a resource surplus. Without a surplus, a business project would only end up as a "go-between" and with a negative balance, it would be a value destroyer.

"It's the business model, stupid!"

E very startup or innovation project has to have a business model, except that we're not always aware of it. To describe and optimize a business model, it has to be clear how value is created, how value is captured, and what is needed to deliver the value that was created.[35] Business Model Canvas has proven to be effective at describing the business model,[36] as it neatly positions the most important building blocks and clearly displays them on a single page. The nine Business Model Canvas building blocks are explained in detail on page 56 et seq.

WHAT DOES A BUSINESS MODEL DESCRIBE?

Every product and company thus has a model describing how the business is operated. If we become more aware of it and also try to differentiate ourselves in how we operate the business, further innovation sources will reveal themselves to us. In addition to product and service innovation, this so-called business model innovation has also grown in importance in the past few years. For example, the Uber taxi service did not change taxi driving, it changed how taxi businesses operate.

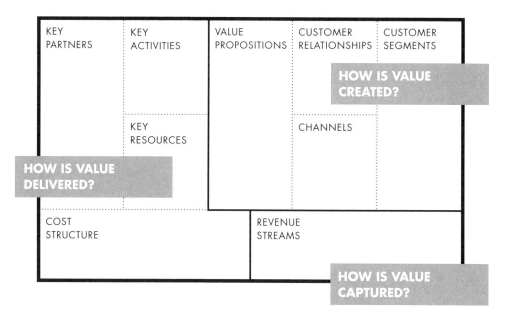

The three key guiding questions to describe a business model

T he viability of a business model has two parts. On the one hand, our solution has to create a value for the customer that is perceived as being higher than the price they have to pay for it. In other words, the value we deliver with our solution has to be higher for the customer than the value we capture through the revenue (or other values, like data, for example). If this is the case, we've cleared the first hurdle to viability: <u>A viable monetization model (Viability 1)</u>.

BUSINESS MODEL VIABILITY

On the other hand, a startup or innovation project is only worthwhile if we can deliver the solution efficiently enough so that our costs are lower than the revenue and we make a profit. To generate profit, we have to clear the second hurdle to viability: <u>A viable operating model (Viability 2)</u>.[37]

VIABLE BUSINESS MODEL

Created value > captured value > delivered value
      MONETIZATION   OPERATING MODEL

In the case of non-profit projects, profit might not take center stage, but costs still need to be covered. And not every non-profit project has a business model. It's the source and type of financing that differentiates them from commercial projects.

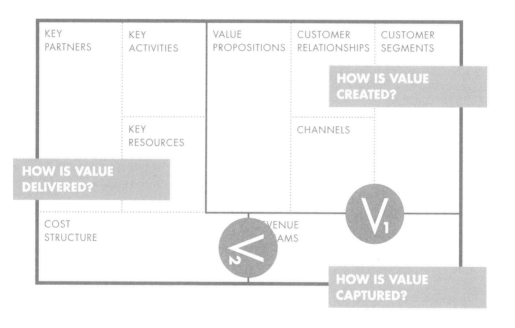

The viability of a business model has two parts

T he term monetization describes whether and how the delivered value—in the form of a solution—can generate revenue.
The viability of the monetization model is determined via three
factors and their respective questions: How easily and efficiently
can we acquire new customers? How high is the monetization
per customer and how often does it take place? How long can we
retain the customers?

VIABILITY 1: VIABLE MONETIZATION MODEL

ATTAINABILITY

Efficiently acquiring and supplying new customers is essential
to the success of a product or service. The more easily potential
customers can be reached and convinced to buy our offering,
the more viable our monetization model will be. The acquisition
and distribution costs have to be significantly lower than the
customer's lifetime value. In addition, qualitative analyses can
be conducted to find out how easily potential customers can be
reached and won over. For example, a very specific customer group
would be easier to reach via specialist media than a very broad
customer group.

AMOUNT AND REPEATABILITY

The absolute amount of revenue per customer is instrumental in determining how viable the monetization model is. An additional, oft-forgotten aspect is repeatability. The offering should deliver an added value that isn't just a one-off; it should be in demand over and over again. When repeatability increases, the lifetime value per customer also increases. Positive examples are the business of everyday groceries or haircuts. Both problems (hunger, hair that needs cutting) need to be solved over and over again. An example of an absence of repeatability would be toys, which are only in vogue for a very short time, like the digital pet, Tamagotchi. The monetization might be very high in the short term, but the demand is not repeatable. So we need to ask ourselves if the customers will purchase and use our offering regularly, or whether it's a one-time opportunity.

SUSTAINABILITY

Just like repeatability, the sustainability of a business model pertains to how long the innovation can hold its own on the market against new, alternative solutions. Ash Maurya calls this the "unfair advantage."[38] We need to ask ourselves how long we can maintain the added value over alternative solutions, and whether we can incorporate some sort of copy protection if needed. The stronger the effect of copy protection, the lower the risk of being ousted by other solutions. Patents or a very big customer base, for example, can help protect you from competitors. In any case, full protection is only possible temporarily, if at all.

T he operating model describes how the value is delivered in the form of the solution. The viability of the operation model is also based on three factors and their respective questions: How easily and well can we implement the business model? How profitably can we operate the business? How motivated are those involved to work in the respective field for months and years?

VIABILITY 2: VIABLE OPERATING MODEL

FEASIBILITY

The operating model needs to be implementable or feasible. On the one hand, specific skills are needed to draft and then run the business model. The capability analysis should describe the actual state and identify possible gaps that can be filled by other team members or external partners.

On the other hand, the startup or innovation project has to be technologically feasible. Depending on the solution, it's possible that the project won't be implemented until after a technological innovation has been developed or after a further general technological development. Here, too, the actual state has to be checked and assessed, to determine how easily and quickly the implementation can occur.

PROFITABILITY

The operating model is viable when we can deliver the created value efficiently enough such that the recovered value is higher than the expenses needed to deliver the value. The basis for calculating profitability is the short- or medium-term revenue potential identified with the success factor "potential." What is important here is that we can be profitable quickly enough so that the business can exist and grow on its own accord. We have to become profitable before we run out of money.

MOTIVATION

In addition to these "hard factors," the motivation to successfully implement and maintain an idea is no less important. The greater our intrinsic interest in an idea's topic, the prospect of an exciting solution and the future satisfaction of potential customers, the greater the energy we'll be able to and want to commit. This is not an insignificant detail, especially since a startup or innovation project can take months and even years.

CAN
WE WAN
OPERATE
B
MODEL

AND DO

T TO

THE

USINESS

?

SUB-QUESTIONS
SUCCESS FACTOR
"VIABILITY"

1 HOW HIGH IS THE POTENTIAL CUSTOMERS' WILLINGNESS TO PAY?

2 HOW EASILY AND EFFICIENTLY CAN WE REACH POTENTIAL CUSTOMERS?

5 IS THE BUSINESS MODEL SUSTAINABLE?

6 HOW WELL CAN WE PROTECT OURSELVES FROM IMITATORS AND COPIES?

9 IS THE OPERATING MODEL EFFICIENT ENOUGH?

10 IS OUR BUSINESS MODEL PROFITABLE ENOUGH?

3 HOW EASILY AND EFFICIENTLY CAN WE CONVINCE POTENTIAL CUSTOMERS TO MAKE A PURCHASE?

4 IS THE BUSINESS MODEL REPEATABLE?

7 DO WE HAVE THE SKILLS AND ENOUGH EXPERIENCE TO DEVELOP AND RUN THE BUSINESS MODEL?

8 IS OUR SOLUTION TECHNOLOGICALLY ACHIEVABLE?

11 IS PROFITABILITY HIGH ENOUGH RELATIVE TO INVESTMENTS?

12 DOES THE OPERATING MODEL MOTIVATE US ENOUGH?

RED

YELLOW

GREEN

NEGATIVE ASSESSMENT OF THE VIABILITY
THE VIABILITY AS A WHOLE, THE MONETIZATION MODEL OR THE OPERATING MODEL ARE ASSESSED AS BEING INSUFFICIENTLY OPTIMISTIC.

If customers are not willing to pay, or not regularly enough, we have to create greater added value. If we can't reach potential customers efficiently enough or if the business model is not lucrative enough overall, we have to make comprehensive changes to the startup or innovation project.

UNCLEAR ASSESSMENT OF THE VIABILITY
WHILE THERE APPEARS TO BE VIABILITY, NOT ALL FACTORS CAN BE ASSESSED CLEARLY OR POSITIVELY ENOUGH.

We have to further analyze one or several factors that describe the viability of the monetization model and the operating model, as we have to further test and optimize the startup and innovation project. For all criteria there is hope that they can still be assessed as positive. All those involved have to agree on what form the positive assessment will take, and when this will happen by.

POSITIVE ASSESSMENT OF THE VIABILITY
ALL FACTORS OF A VIABLE MONETIZATION AND A VIABLE OPERATING MODEL, AND THUS THE VIABILITY OF THE BUSINESS MODEL AS A WHOLE, ARE CLEARLY CATEGORIZED AS POSITIVE.

The "hard" criteria of attainability, amount and repeatability, feasibility and profitability have to be clearly assessable as positive. By contrast, the "soft" criteria of sustainability and motivation are not fully assessable from an objective standpoint, so there is, to a certain degree, some room for interpretation. This is why an assessment of the soft factors should be done by everyone involved in the project.

SCALABL

LITY

SUCCESS FACTOR 5
HOW QUICKLY CAN WE GROW?

The scalability of a startup or innovation project is more than the ability to multiply the offering and to thus be able to grow as a department or a company. A scalable business is not just linear, but also disproportionately capable of growth. In extreme cases, scalable startup or innovation projects are even able to grow exponentially. The companies behind them are therefore called exponential organizations, and by definition, they grow at least ten times faster than the competition.[39]

WHAT IS
SCALABILITY?

Not every offering or company has to be able to grow as significantly and quickly. However, in the field of digitalization, a few companies like Google, Facebook and Uber entered the market and put entire sectors at risk because of their exponential growth. They developed into dominant market powers or even into monopolies. This forces us to better understand scalability opportunities and levers and, if it makes sense, to also harness them.

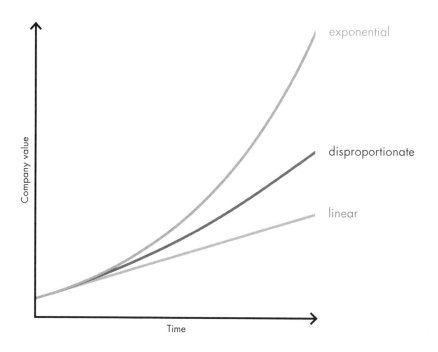

For scalability projects, disproportionate or exponential growth is possible.

I f the business model and its operation are understood as a dynamic system, we will identify a self-reinforcing "mechanism":[40] The higher the created value is for customers, the higher the recovered value, the higher the margins, the higher the potential for reinvestment, the higher the delivered value for customers—a cycle of success that strengthens itself (also known as an upward spiral or a virtuous circle).

SCALING VIA A SELF-REINFORCING MECHANISM IN THE BUSINESS MODEL

A startup or innovation project's general capacity for growth is based on the efficacy of this virtuous circle's self-reinforcing strengths. This is why it stands to reason that scalability should also be analyzed using this idea, in order to find out how well and easily the self-reinforcing strengths can be promoted and accelerated. If we want to optimize scalability, we can start with the mechanism's bottlenecks. This is carried out separately at the respective levers: 1. monetization, 2. the margin, and 3. the attractiveness of the offering. The following pages explain how the scalability of a startup or innovation project can be increased via the three levers.

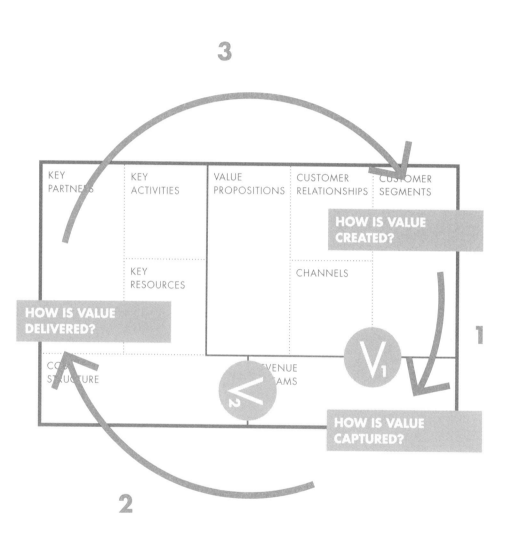

1.
ACCELERATION LEVER: MONETIZATION

2.
ACCELERATION LEVER: MARGIN

3.
ACCELERATION LEVER: ATTRACTIVENESS OF THE OFFERING

Three levers to accelerate the scaling mechanism in a business model

To accelerate the self-reinforcing virtuous circle via monetization, we need to ask ourselves the following question: How can we disproportionately increase sales while decreasing expenses (assuming that we have all the means available to us for customer acquisition and distribution)? In Business Model Canvas, this corresponds to the "Channels" and "Customer relationships" building blocks. The goal behind this is to decrease the marginal costs of acquisition and distribution so that expenses for each new customer also continue to drop.

1. ACCELERATION LEVER: MONETIZATION

To reach this goal, many startup and innovation projects, in addition to relying on the usual acquisition channels described in greater detail in the Traction chapter, rely on automatically distributing their idea through existing users. "Virality" is the magic word that all innovation teams and startups dream of. First, the bad news: Very few products and services are so exciting and prized that they disseminate all on their own. But, the good news is: We can promote virality. For a more in-depth look at virality, I recommend the books "Made to Stick: Why Some Ideas Survive and Others Die," by Chip Heath and Dan Heath[41] and "Contagious: How to Build Word of Mouth in the Digital Age," by Jonah Berger[42]. For example, Berger identifies six attributes that are responsible for more easily and quickly disseminating ideas: 1. social currency thanks to dissemination, 2. dissemination triggers, 3. emotions behind an idea 4. public visibility, 5. practical value and 6. stories that can be disseminated.

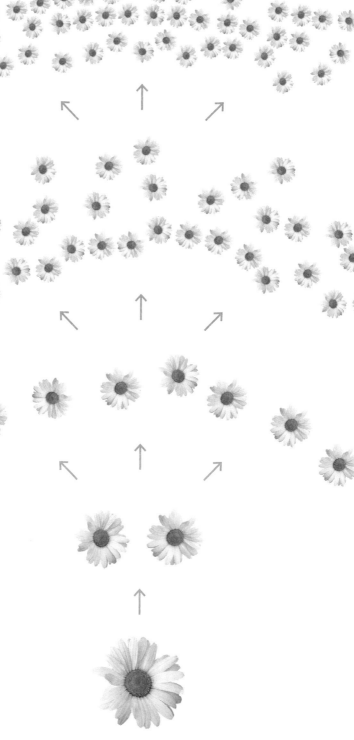

L et's assume that we accelerated monetization and were thus able to disproportionately acquire lots of new customers. We then also have to cushion this as an organization and be able to serve the sharp increase in customers at a high-quality level, so we don't lose existing and new customers and so we can increase the margins. The operating model thus also has to be able to keep up with disproportionate growth and become increasingly efficient. The costs for serving additional customers have to drop disproportionately so that the operating model can really be seen as scalable.

Operating leverage represents an important indicator. The higher the proportion of fixed costs as compared to variable costs, the stronger the operating leverage. In the event of an increase in revenue, the operating costs barely climb, so the operating profit grows disproportionately as compared to revenue. The lower the operational expenses of offering another unit are, the greater the leverage. For example, if a service can be used digitally online, an additional user will cost next to nothing, and marginal costs are next to nothing.

2. ACCELERATION LEVER: MARGIN

In addition, the scalability in an operating model is strongly affected by the degree of automation. For example, the training and support of new Uber drivers are fully automated via videos. Outsourcing production steps also provides another opportunity. Many providers of consumer electronic devices don't manufacture the devices themselves, but have them produced by suppliers, thus outsourcing the challenges connected with scalability.

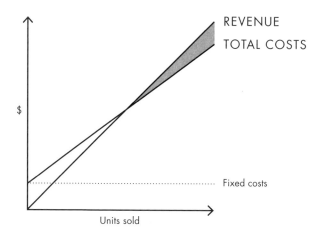

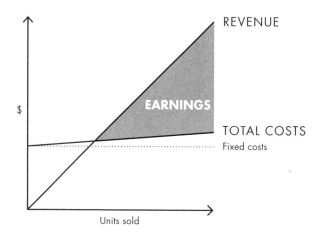

The operating model determines the margin and the operating leverage

T hrough the acceleration of monetization and an efficient operating model, both revenue and profit margins grow disproportionately. As a result, resources are freed up at an ever-increasing rate, and these can be reinvested into the attractiveness of the offering. This closes the cycle, and the value delivered to customers can be progressively enhanced. A prerequisite for this is that we invest resources such that a true added value results for which customers are more willing to pay, more frequently and over a longer period.

3. ACCELERATION LEVER: ATTRACTIVENESS OF THE OFFERING

We have a special scenario when our offering becomes more and more valuable through the growing number of customers and increased use. This results in a so-called network effect, whereby the value of our offering increases not just through our own investments, but also through our users' "investments."[43] For example, the video platform YouTube increases in value the more people upload videos. On the other hand, however, as consumers, we're more likely to look for videos on YouTube than on other provider platforms. The platform has become a standard for videos, resulting in a growing connection between producers and consumers. Another example of the network effect is the Uber taxi service. The more drivers they have, the bigger the geographic coverage, the faster the driver gets to their potential fare, the more people use the service, the more people become drivers.

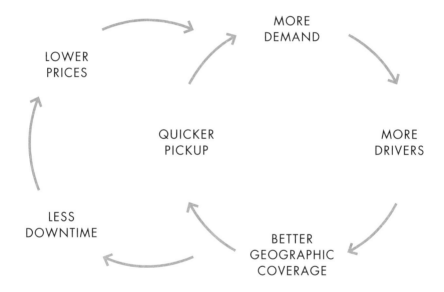

Uber's increased growth through the network effect

I f we define scalability as an organization's disproportionate ability to grow, then certain extreme cases can even grow exponentially.[44] We are assuming a growth rate that is at least ten times larger.

Exponential organizations are characterized by five traits that promote scalability from an internal and external perspective. Externally, these are: (1) an on-demand labor force, (2) a community and an ecosystem that actively support the vision and the mission, (3) an algorithm that can automatically analyze and assess software data, (4) a comprehensive as possible outsourcing of work processes, and (5) customer involvement and loyalty. The internal traits include: (1) automated interfaces allowing customers to interact with the organization as efficiently as possible, (2) a leadership cockpit that portrays the current status of the organization, (3) innovation according to Lean Startup, (4) a high degree of autonomy and self-organization, and (5) digital collaboration tools.

EXTREME CASE: EXPONENTIAL ORGANIZATION

Whether dominant corporations or monopolies are socially appropriate and how we get around traits such as "on-demand labor force" from an ethical and societal viewpoint is subject to further discussion.

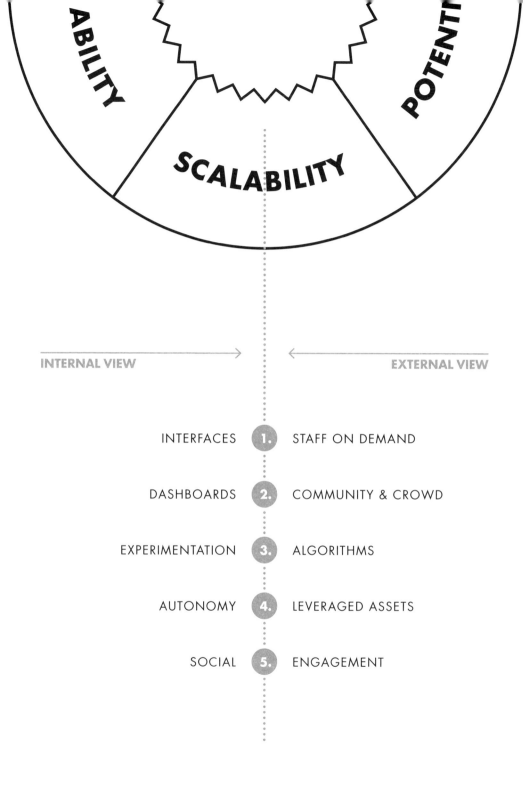

The scaling traits of an exponential organization (Ismail et al., 2014)

A nother extreme case is represented by offerings that are used so regularly and extensively by customers that they become a positive habit or, in a negative case, even become addictive. E-mail, Facebook and Instagram could definitely be counted as some of the best-known examples of this.

EXTREME CASE: HABIT-FORMING PRODUCT

The advantage of being a provider of habit-forming products and services is that usage becomes more extensive on its own, without us having to actively promote it; the attractiveness of the offering therefore scales itself. Nir Eyal developed a model to explain and optimize the self-reinforcement of habit-forming offerings:[45] First, we need to either encourage ourselves or be encouraged to do an activity with the help of a trigger. This is followed by the actual activity, in expectation of the resulting variable gratification. In the end, we actively invest in the solution, but with very little monetary output, so that the next usage will be even more valuable.

If we use Instagram as an example, the process would be as follows: People talk about an Instagram post (trigger). Because this reminds us about Instagram, we open the app (action). We discover a few interesting posts and photos (variable gratification). We really like the photo of a recipe, so we save it to our collection (investment). This increases its value in our eyes. In the evening, when it's time to cook supper, we remember the recipe. Another trigger to scroll through the app again.

The self-reinforcing cycle of habit-forming products (Eyal, 2014)

N ot every product, service or business can be scaled equally. But we should be aware of the degree of scaling we currently have and how scalable we want or even need to be in the future.

DEGREE OF SCALING AS A CONTINUUM AND GOAL-SETTING

The degree of scaling can be understood as a continuum. We can situate our current and future position on this continuum. We should always ask whether and how we can increase our scalability. Digitalization and questioning related solutions don't only have to do with new technologies, but also with changed scaling opportunities in particular. Nowadays, new competitors don't just offer a digital version of a product or service. The business models of the new competitors are most often highly scalable so that disproportionate or even exponential growth is possible. Only in this way can related sectors be disruptively changed after just a few years, so fully turned upside down. Therefore, this competition does not just take place via the superficial technology, as is so often readily depicted, but also via the degree of scaling.

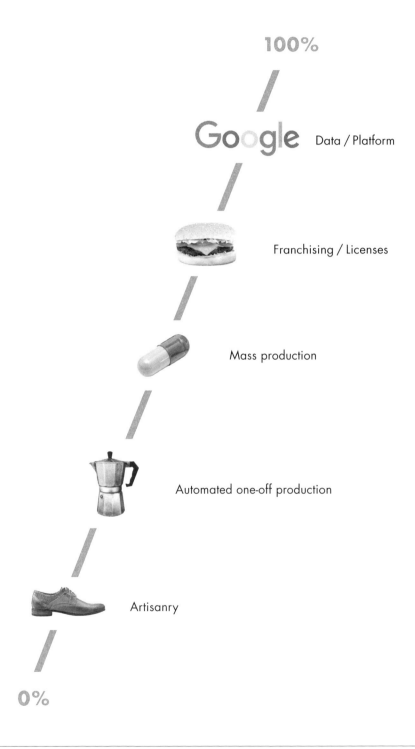

The degree of scaling varies depending on the solution and the business model

MAIN QUESTION
SUCCESS FACTOR
"SCALABILITY"

QUICKLY

EFFICIEN

WE GRO

HOW

AND

TLY CAN

W ?

1 HOW CAN WE ACCELERATE AND AUTOMATE THE DISTRIBUTION AND DISSEMINATION OF OUR OFFERING?

2 HOW CAN WE CONTINUOUSLY LOWER ACQUISITION AND DISTRIBUTION COSTS?

5 WHICH AREAS OF THE OPERATING MODEL CAN WE AUTOMATE?

6 WHICH AREAS OF THE OPERATING MODEL CAN WE OUTSOURCE AND MAKE MORE FLEXIBLE?

9 WHAT FEATURES OF AN EXPONENTIAL ORGANIZATION CAN WE ADOPT?

10 HOW CAN WE MAKE THE USAGE OF OUR OFFERING ROUTINE?

3 HOW CAN WE TAKE ADVANTAGE OF THE POTENTIAL OF VIRAL DISSEM- INATION?

4 HOW CAN WE EFFICIENTLY SERVE RAPIDLY RISING DEMAND?

7 HOW CAN WE CONTINUOUSLY INCREASE CUSTOMERS' LIFETIME VALUE?

8 HOW CAN WE BENEFIT FROM NETWORK EFFECTS?

11 WHICH BOTTLE- NECKS IN THE BUSINESS MODEL'S SELF-REINFORCING "MECHANISM" COULD HALT GROWTH?

12 HAVE WE IDENTIFIED AND HARNESSED ALL SCALING POTENTIAL?

RED

YELLOW

GREEN

NEGATIVE ASSESSMENT OF SCALABILITY
THE BUSINESS MODEL INDICATES INSUFFICIENTLY HIGH SCALABILITY OR IT CAN'T BE FULLY TAPPED INTO.

If applicable, scalability can be increased through changes to the solution and in the business model.

UNCLEAR ASSESSMENT OF SCALABILITY
THE BUSINESS MODEL'S SELF-REINFORCING "MECHANISM" CAN BE ACCELERATED VIA AT LEAST ONE OF THE THREE LEVERS (MONETIZATION, MARGIN, ATTRACTIVENESS OF THE OFFERING).

It's still not clear whether and how this acceleration can be implemented. Plus, we need to try to also make acceleration happen through the other levers.

POSITIVE ASSESSMENT OF SCALABILITY
THE BUSINESS MODEL'S SELF-REINFORCING "MECHANISM" CAN BE ACCELERATED VIA ALL THREE LEVERS (MONETIZATION, MARGIN, ATTRACTIVENESS OF THE OFFERING).

The successful harnessing of scalability seems to be very realistic. However, the concrete implementation and its effect have to be continuously checked against growth.

TRACTIO

SUCCESS FACTOR 6
HOW POSITIVELY DO CUSTOMERS REACT?

2

T he success factor "traction" takes center stage in our model, because it reflects the result of our design decisions in the external area of the model. The term comes from the transportation sector and describes the traction and power used by a locomotive to pull railway cars. In the startup and innovation field, this term refers to the "tensile force" exerted by users and customers. This tensile force, or traction, shows how strongly the startup or innovation project triggers a concrete demand and is thus assessed as truly valuable and beneficial by customers. In an ideal case, increasingly more people start showing interest in the offering and using it. In other words, it is quantitative proof of market demand.

WHAT IS
TRACTION?

However, this proof of demand is not just to be checked and proven once. It always has to be proven again because, for a new offering, demand has to grow continuously so that we can assess the traction as positive. We could also talk about momentum, which has to come from the market and proves that the startup or innovation project is gaining speed.

I n the Lean Progress Model, the assessment of traction changes depending on the development status of the project and has to be reestablished with each phase. Traction differs fundamentally from the remaining elements of the model. The five success factors explained up to this point depict our input, so our design decisions. By contrast, traction describes the result (output), so the result of our design decisions.

TRACTION DEPENDS ON THE DEVELOPMENT STATUS

Traction is expressed in various phases of the startup or innovation project through different measured values and needs to be defined accordingly as an indicator: In the first phase (problem-solution fit), customers often can't yet use the offering and generate revenue respectively. Nevertheless, this phase is already about potential customers starting to independently and actively show interest in the offering. They start to show their interest, creating market pull. Instead of using money, they "pay" using other valuable resources, like their time or their e-mail address. At the latest in the second phase (product-market fit), customers obtain the offering in exchange for money, which means we can measure revenue in financial terms. In this phase, we want to assess whether just a few early adopters are interested or whether a larger client base can be developed, so whether it's a real market. If the latter is proven to be the case, traction shows in the third phase (scaling) whether the speed of growth can be increased in the success factor "scalability" according to the assessment.

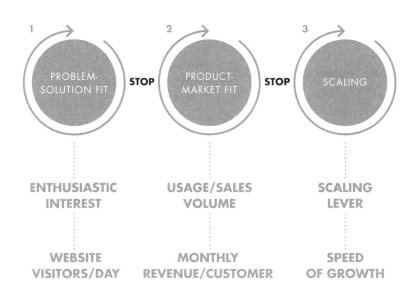

Changes to the traction category in the Lean Innovation process

T he indicators to measure traction depend on the type of solution and the sector. For example, indicators for an offering for private end-users and an offering for corporate customers vary greatly. For private end-users, approximately 100,000 active users are needed in order to be able to talk about a real market, whereas in the corporate customer environment, just three to four comprehensive projects with corporations can indicate the existence of an attractive market. These values are based on empirical values and show how the existence of demand has to be proven for an investment of a million dollars.[46]

TRACTION DEPENDS ON THE SOLUTION CATEGORY

The solution category also indicates which type of traction is to be measured. For example, an offering in the field of social media relies on having as many customers as possible spend as long as possible and be as active as possible on a platform and exchanging ideas, whereas, in the field of e-commerce, monthly revenue per customer and per category are at the forefront.

PRIVATE CUSTOMERS
**1 MILLION REGISTRATIONS,
100,000 ACTIVE USERS**

CORPORATE CUSTOMERS
**1,000 CUSTOMERS AT
$10 PER MONTH**

CORPORATE CUSTOMERS
(CORPORATIONS)
**2–3 PAID PILOT
PROJECTS**

$1 MILLION
INVESTMENT
CAPITAL

PLATFORM
OR E-COMMERCE
$50,000 REVENUE PER MONTH

The traction objectives are different depending on the solution category (Status: 2013)

W e run the risk of losing ourselves in a sea of metrics. The successful observation and measurement of traction require as strong a focus as possible. It is recommended that we, if we can, limit ourselves to a single indicator which best measures the traction from the market according to the current development phase. As explained on the previous pages, the indicator also depends on the solution category.

THE ONE INDICATOR

We can once again use the bottom-up calculation as suggested for the success factor "potential" as the generally valid and simplified way of measuring traction:[47]

1. Define the minimum but most ambitious performance target in x years. For example: after three years, a revenue of 10 million dollars per year.

2. Translate the minimum performance target to an influenceable throughput indicator. Example: Through the planned annual revenue, the designated 10 million dollars per year are divided per customer, which results in the targeted number of active customers. With a revenue of 1,000 dollars per customer per year, this results in 10,000 active customers in the third year.

3. Extrapolate backward following the three phases of the Lean Innovation process by dividing by 10 for each phase as the simplest approximation for the target values you need to achieve for the second phase, "product-market fit," and the first phase, "problem-solution fit" (see diagram on facing page).

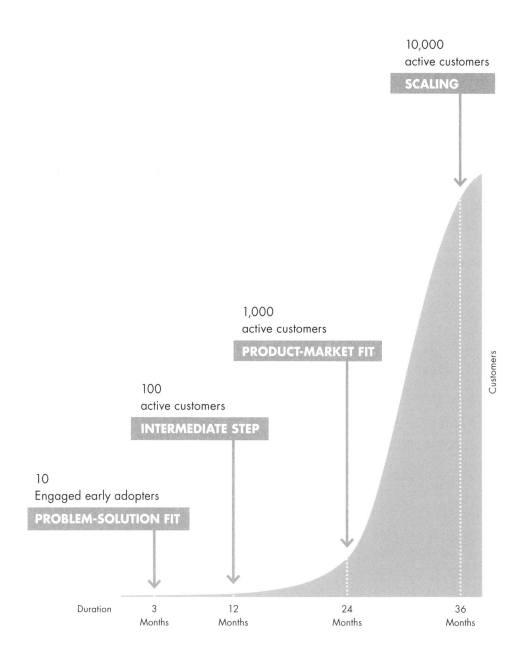

Using the bottom-up calculation for a generically applicable traction indicator
of active customers

GOOD AND BAD
INDICATORS

The field of Lean Innovation differentiates between good and bad indicators.[48] Bad indicators are called "vanity metrics." This includes, for example, the total number of registered users or completed downloads. These numbers can only climb because they're calculated cumulatively. They give you a good feeling. But they don't allow us to draw any meaningful conclusions for the future. A good indicator would be more likely to measure the speed at which the number of new customers is rising and how this speed changes. On this basis, the effect of acquisition measures can be measured and the insight can be used to predict future measures.

GOOD INDICATORS

SHOW THE HEARD REALITY
They help to actively
optimize

ARE EXPLORATIVE
Help identify as yet unknown
contributing factors

**ARE BASED ON A CAUSAL
RELATIONSHIP**
Show the effect of
improvement measures

PREDICTABLE
Help predict the effect
of improvements

BAD INDICATORS

FLATTER
Give you a good feeling,
because they climb

ARE DESCRIPTIVE
Explain what is known

**CORRELATE WITHOUT
CAUSALITY**
It remains unclear which
measures should be enforced

EXPLAIN THE PAST
They might not simply
be bad, but they can no
longer be influenced

E ven an extremely valuable, beneficial offering doesn't just disseminate all on its own. We have to actively contribute towards getting potential customers to find out about our offering and try it out with as little cost as possible. Traction, therefore, doesn't happen on its own, it needs to be actively supported.

FIND THE MOST EFFECTIVE TRACTION CHANNEL

As part of the success factor "viability," we test, among others, how efficiently we can obtain new customers and whether we can organize distribution efficiently enough. We also want to find out which acquisition channels can directly influence traction, and how strong this impact is. For time-related and financial reasons, in the beginning, we can usually only manage one channel intensively enough. That's why it's worth finding the most effective, decisive traction channel through experimentation. The authors Weinberg and Mares suggest proceeding as follows:[49] All 19 potential traction channels are conceptually played out in order to reduce the selection to four to five channels (see image on the next double-page spread). These then have to be tested for efficiency and effectiveness using quick and cost-effective experiments. The experiments should reveal the most effective channel so that our acquisitions happen as efficiently as possible and by combing resources. Just like using a sieve, the process helps us discover which channel loses the least amount of marketing money.[50]

Which traction channel gives us the lowest dispersion losses?

19 POTENTIAL TRACTION CHANNELS

1.
TRADITIONAL PR

2.
UNCONVENTIONAL PR

3.
SEARCH ENGINE MARKETING (SEM)

4.
SEARCH ENGINE OPTIMIZATION (SEO)

5.
SOCIAL MEDIA ADS

6.
E-MAIL MARKETING

7.
VIRAL MARKETING

8.
BUSINESS DEVELOPMENT

9.
OTHERS' BLOGS

10.
CONTENT MARKETING

11.
COMMUNITY BUILDING

12.
TRADESHOW

13.
PRESENTATIONS

14.
USE EXISTING PLATFORMS

15.
PERSONAL SALES

16.
OFFLINE EVENTS

17.
OFFLINE ADVERTISING

18.
PARTNER MARKETING (AFFILIATE-PROGRAMM)

19.
PRODUCT DEVELOPMENT AS MARKETING

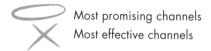

Most promising channels
Most effective channels

IS THE TRACTION ENOUG

MARKET

N

STRONG

H ?

SUB-QUESTIONS
SUCCESS FACTOR
"TRACTION"

1 WHICH INDI-
CATORS AND TARGETS
ARE TYPICAL TO OUR
SECTOR AND SOLUTION
CATEGORY?

2 WHICH "ONE
INDICATOR" ARE WE
CURRENTLY USING
MOST TO MEASURE
TRACTION?

5 DO ALL TEAM
MEMBERS AND
STAKEHOLDERS
UNDERSTAND THE
INDICATORS WELL
ENOUGH?

6 DO WE KNOW WHAT
WE CAN CHANGE TO
INCREASE TRACTION?

9 WHAT REVENUE
GOAL DO
WE WANT TO
ACHIEVE IN
THREE YEARS?

10 HOW MANY
ACTIVE CUSTOMERS
DO WE NEED TO
REACH THIS IN THE
THIRD YEAR?

3 WHICH ADDITIONAL INDICATORS HELP US ASSESS TRACTION EVEN BETTER?

4 ARE OUR INDICATORS EXPLORATIVE, CAUSAL AND PREDICTABLE?

7 WHICH 3 TO 5 CHANNELS PROMISE TO HAVE THE BIGGEST IMPACT ON TRACTION?

8 WHICH SINGLE TRACTION CHANNEL CURRENTLY CONTRIBUTES THE GREATEST IMPROVEMENT, ACCORDING TO EXPERIMENTATION?

11 BASED ON THIS, HOW MANY CUSTOMERS DO WE HAVE TO ACQUIRE IN THE FIRST YEAR?

12 IS THE MARKET TRACTION INCREASING QUICKLY ENOUGH?

RED

YELLOW

GREEN

NEGATIVE ASSESSMENT OF TRACTION
MARKET DEMAND IS TOO LOW TO CONTINUE.

We need to investigate whether and in what form we should and can continue. Optimizing the traction channels should result in a relatively quick and notable improvement. If not, the offering or the startup or innovation project needs to be called into question as a whole.

UNCLEAR ASSESSMENT OF TRACTION
WHILE THERE IS A CERTAIN MARKET DEMAND, WE'RE NOT ACHIEVING THE TARGET VALUES WE'VE SET.

We need to find out whether this is due to the basic configuration of the offering and the business model, or the optimization of the traction channels, and how we can reach the target values we've set.

POSITIVE ASSESSMENT OF TRACTION
WE ARE ACHIEVING OR EXCEEDING THE TARGET VALUES WE'VE SET.

Market demand is gaining momentum and is continuously climbing. We need to find out why this is so and which levers we can use to further strengthen and accelerate growth.

APPLYING
THE
MODEL

THE MODEL IN THE STARTUP AND INNOVATION PROCESS

N ow e've reached the point of being able to apply the Lean Progress Model, through which major added value continues to unfold. In my work as a consultant and a coach, it's been proven that the Lean Innovation process, with the help of the model, runs much better, more quickly, and is more lean. You can use the Lean Progress Model in workshops and meetings without a lot of extra effort. You can either draw the model yourself, or you can use a poster template, which you can find on our website:

www.leaninnovationguide.com

Using a three-step traffic light system, you can assess the progress of the six success factors. The colors are selected as illustrated on the facing page and are determined according to the explanations, guiding questions and assessment templates in the second part of the book.

OFFLINE APPLICATION
USING POST-IT NOTES

Assign the traffic light colors using colored post-it notes or colored paper. What is key is that the color scheme remains flexible. Never write directly on the poster, but only on the post-it notes or the paper.

In addition to assessing progress, the model is used to help guide the Lean Innovation experiments and the respective hypotheses. It is recommended that per one- to two-week test cycle, no more than three hypotheses be defined that currently represent the biggest risks of failure. The hypotheses make it possible to proceed and conduct purposeful tests. The current status of each hypothesis is also recorded on a post-it note.

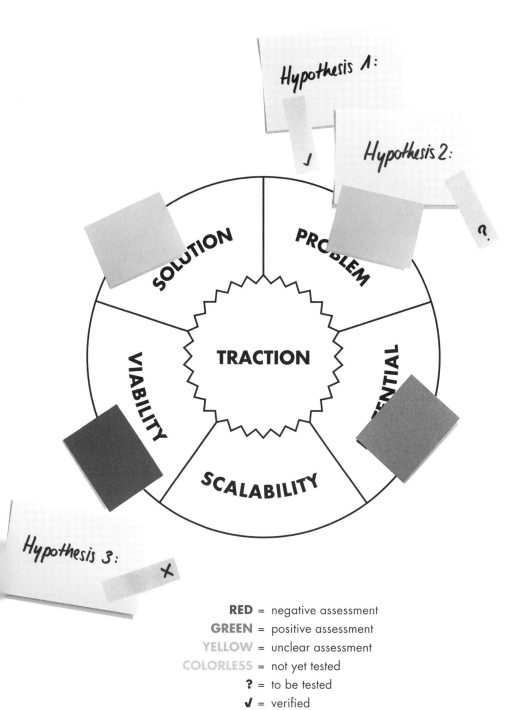

RED = negative assessment
GREEN = positive assessment
YELLOW = unclear assessment
COLORLESS = not yet tested
? = to be tested
√ = verified
X = falsified

T he Lean Progress Model can also be digitally illustrated. You can either digitize the poster afterwards by taking a photo, or you can use a digital version of the model, allowing you to also record discussions, populating the model and optimization on your computer.

DIGITAL
APPLICATION

A key added value of the model is making process progress visible and thereby accelerating and improving the testing in the process. For this, the various test cycles and the ensuing modifications also need to be transparent later on. That is why it is worth illustrating the different stages of the model, even if it's just a rudimentary outline. There are three options available for this: Photos of the posters, a digital template, or the web-based application of the model.

You can download a digital template of the model from our website and find out the current status of a web-based application of the model:

www.leaninnovationguide.com

The model is available for free at any time as a poster and a digital template for your startup, innovation, consulting or training process. If you want to digitally map the model and integrate it into a software package (for example, as part of an innovation and project management software package, as the template for an online whiteboard or something similar), you will need the appropriate license.[51]

TAKING PHOTOS OF THE POSTERS

Easy, convenient, makes use of the creative advantage of offline processing Not very user-friendly, collaboration independent of time and location not possible, static representation

DIGITAL TEMPLATE

Relatively easy, convenient, digitization already occurs during processing Not very user-friendly, collaboration independent of time and location not possible, static representation

THE MODEL AS A DIGITAL SERVICE

Very user friendly, additional functionality possible (e.g.: portfolio function), ideal for collaborations independent of time and place **+ —** Takes time to learn, login might be needed, interactive processing and discussion can be omitted

A nother advantage of the Lean Progress Model is that the development process and the progress of several projects can be followed simultaneously and be compared against each other. This is particularly important if an investment budget is to be divided among several sub-projects and the investments are paid out in installments based on progress according to Lean Startup. It is recommended to first only support interesting ideas with a small budget of 1,000 to 5,000 dollars. This first investment installment has to be enough to check the problem-solution fit. Further investments depend on whether the problem-solution fit is achieved and if so, how convincingly it can be proven.

PORTFOLIO REPRESENTATION POSSIBLE

In most cases, an internal and external perspective define the position of the startup and innovation projects in the portfolio view. The expected potential and the likelihood of success determine how high-risk an investment has to be, or what its likelihood of success has to be. We can draw the minimum and optimum risk-potential-relationship in the graphical representation of the portfolio. Based on the assessment in the Lean Progress Model, each project is given a current position in the portfolio. Color coding makes the projects easier to compare and manage.

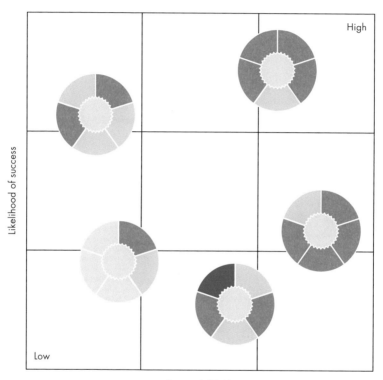

Portfolio representation using the Lean Progress Model

I deally, the success factors within the model are checked and optimized according to the order in which they're depicted, which also corresponds to the order in which they appear in this book. First, the success factor "problem" is tested, then the success factor "solution," followed by the success factor "potential," and so on. This doesn't mean that a success factor first needs to have a green—or positive—assessment before you move on to the next success factor. We can see the order as an iterative process that is gone through over and over again. With every round, knowledge and clarity grow as to how the project's chances of success are to be assessed.

IDEAL-TYPICAL SEQUENCE IN THE MODEL

In any case, prioritizing risks dictates which hypotheses are to be tested first. However, there is a certain trend whereby risk prioritization also corresponds to the ideal sequence in the model: If, for example, the problem isn't relevant enough, a solution becomes obsolete. If a solution doesn't contribute any true added value to alternative solutions, then there's no potential to tap into, either. If the potential isn't interesting enough, there's no reason to check viability. If we don't assess the viability as positive, then there's no scalability to harness.

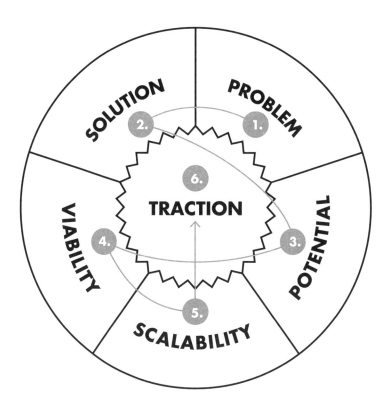

The ideal-typical order of success factors in the iterative discovery and learning process

T he three-step, linear, Lean Innovation process can be per-
fectly linked to the model and synchronized. What is important is that we constantly check the type of traction indicator and adapt it, if necessary, if we don't limit ourselves to
measuring the generally applicable number of customers. At
the beginning we might measure how quickly newsletter sign-
ups increase, but later, the change in monthly revenue per customer will more likely take center stage in our analysis. In addition, the success factor "traction" should be identified as not
yet tested at the start of each phase, in order to measure the
requirements dependent on the phase.

THE MODEL IN THE LEAN INNOVATION PROCESS

Depending on the phase of the Lean Innovation process, positive
proof of the model's success factors has to be demonstrated:

1. PROBLEM-SOLUTION FIT

At the very least, the success factors "problem" and "solution" as
well as the appropriate traction indicator have to be positively
assessed and proven.

2. PRODUCT-MARKET FIT

In addition, the success factors "potential" and "viability" as well
as the adapted traction indicator have to be assessed as positive.

3. SCALING

While scaling has to be assessed as potentially positive as early
as possible, it can't actually be proven until this third phase, if
need be.

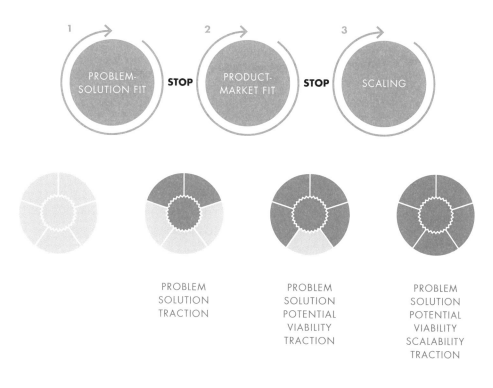

The Lean Progress Model in the Lean Innovation process

M ost larger companies and some SMEs have already defined an individual innovation process, adapted to the organizational characteristics. Even if the companies have already partially or fully aligned the process according to Lean Innovation, some deviate from the three-phase problem-solution fit, product-market fit and scaling.

THE MODEL IN
ADAPTED INNOVATION
PROCESSES

The top images show what a modified process could look like. The innovation process is from a book in which the authors adapted the innovation process according to Lean Startup.[52] The Lean Progress Model can be used for this and all other imaginable innovation processes. We only need to be aware of which success factors of the Lean Progress Model we focus our analysis, testing and optimization on, and in which phase of the respective process.

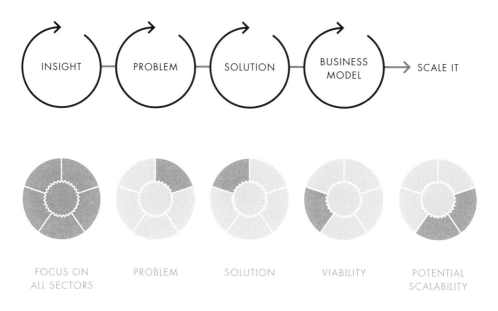

Using the Lean Progress Model for adapted innovation processes

T he advantage of a Lean approach according to Lean Innovation lies in avoiding waste—that is, not incurring any unnecessary investments—and in finding out as quickly and as purposefully as possible whether a startup or innovation project will be successful on the market, how it needs to be modified if required, and whether it should be shelved in favor of another project.

LEAN INNOVATION LEADERSHIP

Even if we develop the innovation process this way, we tend to fall in love with the first ideas and end up focusing on the solution or the development of a functional and pretty product, instead of questioning the problem and its solution. That is why Lean Innovation leadership—the task of the people leading this process—consists of constantly promoting and also insisting on truly Lean processes in terms of content, time and finances.

INNOVATION MANAGEMENT VIA RISK PRIORITIZATION

From an innovation point of view, it is essential to start by checking the biggest and most urgent risks using the definition of respective hypotheses and by conducting tests. Lean is when we investigate and minimize the biggest risks right at the outset. We recommend keeping a dynamic catalog of hypotheses (called backlog in agile terminology) and to regularly check the prioritization and integrity of the catalog. Accurate risk prioritization is the be-all and end-all of Lean processes.

TIME MANAGEMENT USING TIMEBOXING

From a time perspective, the learning process has to happen quickly and purposefully. The leadership role is to create a certain amount of pressure, without overwhelming or demotivating the team. An ambitious schedule should be set up for each test cycle with those involved. We split up the learning process within set periods—so-called timeboxes. For example, we might check the three current high-risk and open-ended hypotheses every two weeks.

FINANCIAL MANAGEMENT VIA STAGGERED INVESTMENTS

Traditionally, financial resources were invested based on the expected return on investment according to calculations in the business plan. However, from a Lean Innovation perspective, we should create the incentive to learn as much and as quickly as possible with as few resources as possible. Staggering investments and making them dependent on progress is thus recommended. However, there is a risk that the projects are also represented too positively, even according to the Lean approach, to access new investment funds. To prevent this, open communication with all those involved is required, on the one hand, and on the other hand, successful project cancellations can be rewarded with a bonus payment of sorts, which will flow into the development of a new, better project.

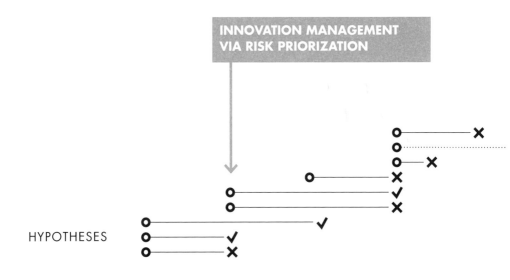

**INNOVATION MANAGEMENT
VIA RISK PRIORIZATION**

HYPOTHESES

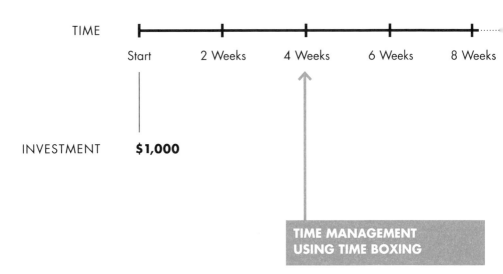

TIME

Start   2 Weeks   4 Weeks   6 Weeks   8 Weeks

INVESTMENT   **$1,000**

**TIME MANAGEMENT
USING TIME BOXING**

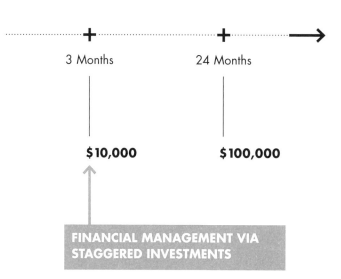

The three Lean Innovation leadership guiding principles

A ssuming you were able to test and optimize the overall direction of the startup or innovation project to such an extent that the customers are already paying for a minimum viable product, then product or service development can be continued. The expenses and complexity can grow substantially. In 2017, approximately 1,000 people were working on product development for the social media app Snapchat;[53] over 16,000 employees make up the Uber taxi service, a fairly substantial number.[54] The continuous further development of a product and coordinating all people involved is a challenging leadership task. Here we need to differentiate between investigative tasks and tasks with a clear result, both of which need to be synchronized. In other words, we need to establish a balance while also carefully coordinating innovation- and implementation-oriented tasks.

LEAN PRODUCT MANAGEMENT

Innovation-oriented tasks include, for example, the development of new functionalities for existing products and services. We can also explore and optimize these tasks following the six success factors in the model. The process continues to be managed while taking content-related, temporal and financial aspects into consideration.

INNOVATION MANAGEMENT: FOCUSING THANKS TO "OBJECTIVES AND KEY RESULTS (OKR)"

With the continuous further development of products and services, it's important to restrict this work to bigger issues over a specific timeframe. Companies like Intel, Google or Twitter use an interesting methodology called OKR, which stands for Objectives and Key Results.[55] Ambitious goals are set for a three-month period to establish what should be improved for the customers and why, and how progress is to be measured. This directs the activities of all those involved and makes it possible to constantly check the status at any given moment.

TIME MANAGEMENT: TIMEBOXING FOLLOWING AGILE PRODUCT DEVELOPMENT

A certain time constraint is also required for optimization and continuous further development. In the context of OKR methodology, this is usually three months, However, the required activities have to be broken down into smaller units of time. If you implement an agile product development process like scrum, the innovation- and implementation-oriented activities should be integrated, but also kept distinct. You can illustrate this in the scrum process by using different colors on the kanban board, for example (see diagram on the next double-page spread).

FINANCIAL MANAGEMENT: BUDGETING BASED ON THE USER STORY

The allocation of temporal and financial resources should follow the development cycles (sprints). The weighting is decided based on the estimated amount of work for the task. It can make sense here to have a set capacity allocation. For example, every sprint could plan for an average of one third of the capacity for innovation-oriented tasks.

PRODUCT BACKLOG	SPRINT BACKLOG	IN PROGRESS
USER STORY	USER STORY / TASK / TASK	TASK
USER STORY / USER STORY	USER STORY / TASK / TASK	TASK
USER STORY		
USER STORY		

TO BE TESTED   COMPLETED

innovation-oriented
implementation-oriented

The kanban board in Lean product management

I n his book, "Lean Startup," Eric Ries identifies ten general types of pivots.[56] They highlight how startup and innovation projects can fundamentally change in order to increase their chance of success. The pivots are summarized below:

GENERAL TYPES
OF PIVOTS

1. Zoom-in: A single feature of a whole package becomes a product
2. Zoom-out: A single feature is expanded, becoming a whole package
3. Customer segment: A previously unconsidered segment is identified as appropriate
4. Customer need: A problem to be solved changes
5. Platform: Instead of developing a product for products, a platform is developed
6. Business architecture: A change in competitive methods
7. Value capture: A change in the way we deliver, create and recover value
8. Engine of growth: A change to the way in which we accelerate growth
9. Channel: A change in the primary sales and distribution channels
10. Technology: A change in the primary sales and distribution channels

The Lean Progress Model helps us map pivots to success factors.

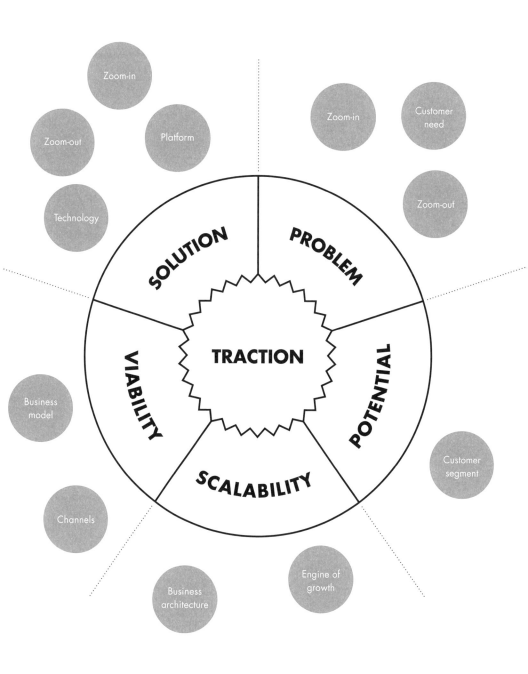

Ten possible pivots and where they're situated in the Lean Progress Model
(according to Ries, 2011)

E ver since the Lean Innovation movement was set in motion, many more methods, models, frameworks and tools have come to be. Older methods like Design Thinking are also often associated with Lean Innovation.[57] Quite often it's not methods we're lacking, it's clarity as to why, when and with what objective these are to be implemented. The Lean Progress Model serves as a guide for your method toolkit. It's a meta-model that can be used to categorize and better explain the other methods.

THE MODEL AS A NAVIGATIONAL AID FOR OTHER METHODS

The image on the facing page shows a few other Lean Innovation methods and where they fit in. In order to not go beyond the scope of this book, these methods will not be described in detail here. There are numerous, easy-to-find books and websites on these methods.

The next chapter applies this model to a case study to illustrate how a startup or innovation project can continuously transform.

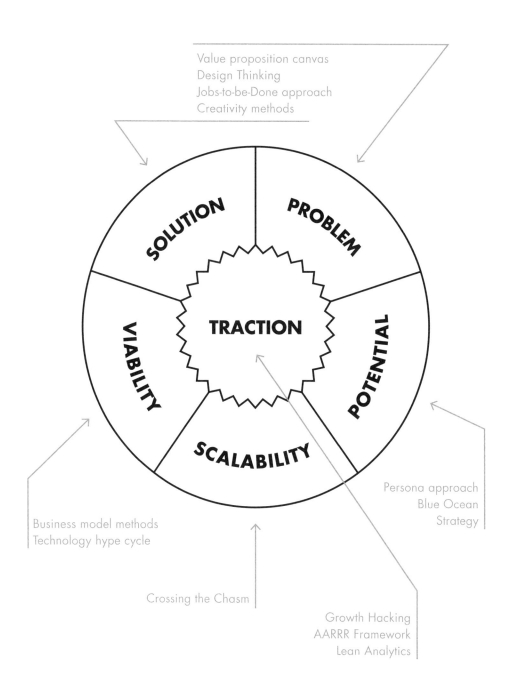

Value proposition canvas
Design Thinking
Jobs-to-be-Done approach
Creativity methods

SOLUTION

PROBLEM

VIABILITY

TRACTION

POTENTIAL

SCALABILITY

Persona approach
Blue Ocean
Strategy

Business model methods
Technology hype cycle

Crossing the Chasm

Growth Hacking
AARRR Framework
Lean Analytics

The Lean Progress Model situates and further explains additional methods

CASE STUDY

"EMPTY SPACE EXCHANGE"

INTRODUCTION

This chapter will illustrate the implementation and added value of the Lean Progress Model using a concrete innovation project as an example. The model serves as a guide for the open-ended questions, test results and assessment of the success factors for the case study's respective test and optimization cycles.

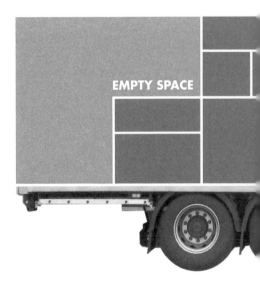

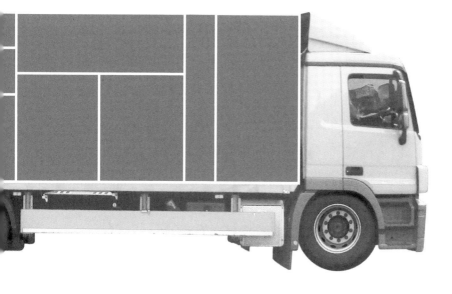

INITIAL IDEA:
EMPTY SPACE EXCHANGE IN THE LOGISTICS SECTOR

An innovation team started with the idea of a digital platform that offers the private sector inexpensive empty space with logistic companies. For example, a private person wants to send their scooter from Germany to their vacation rental in Spain. This is relatively expensive. Using the empty space exchange, the person could locate a truck that is traveling to the desired city or area in Spain and still has space for the scooter. The private person could have this item shipped at half the usual cost. The logistics company could bring in additional revenue for a trip that is going to take place anyway. It's a classic win-win situation. Or is it?

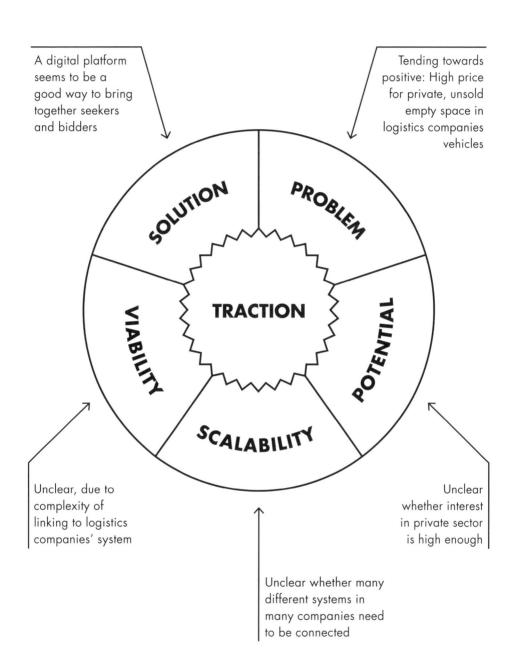

A digital platform seems to be a good way to bring together seekers and bidders

Tending towards positive: High price for private, unsold empty space in logistics companies vehicles

SOLUTION

PROBLEM

VIABILITY

TRACTION

POTENTIAL

SCALABILITY

Unclear, due to complexity of linking to logistics companies' system

Unclear whether interest in private sector is high enough

Unclear whether many different systems in many companies need to be connected

FIRST ITERATION:
DISAPPOINTMENT

The innovation team decides to conduct interviews right away, to get real responses from the market as quickly as possible. First they take their empty space idea and approach logistics companies, as they would be key partners and thus instrumental to the implementation of their idea. After just one week, they're met with disappointment: Logistics companies don't have empty space. Thanks to planning software, they can and need to eliminate inefficiencies like this. This is good for the logistics companies, but also for the innovation team, Because the sooner the team can identify which aspects of their idea will work and which won't, the sooner their limited resources can be used towards optimized aspects or more promising ideas.

Makes no sense without a relevant problem

Logistics companies have no empty space and don't have this problem

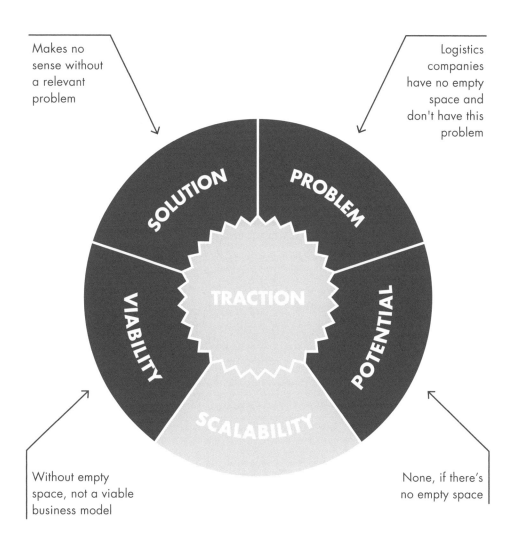

Without empty space, not a viable business model

None, if there's no empty space

SECOND ITERATION:
ON TO NEW HORIZONS

The innovation team members are a bit disappointed, but hold onto their central vision of wanting to introduce a revolutionary or at least noteworthy innovation to the transportation sector. The innovation team not only pivots, but develops a completely different idea: a peer-to-peer system for transporting packages. Their idea is that train commuters could pick up a package at the train station and hand it off when they transfer trains or reach their final destination. The commuters would receive a small payment in exchange. This idea also seems creative at first glance, even if implementing it would be challenging.

To test the idea of peer-to-peer logistics, the innovation team once again conducted interviews. This time, instead of talking to key partners, they approached the train commuters who would take a package with them and earn a bit of extra money in the process. The responses were somewhat less clear this time around. But they did show that train commuters did not have enough interest in taking on the effort of transporting a package in exchange for a bit of extra money. Not least because the package would have to be stowed away on the train, or be kept on the person's lap. And because the pick-up and drop-off would entail additional effort by the commuter.

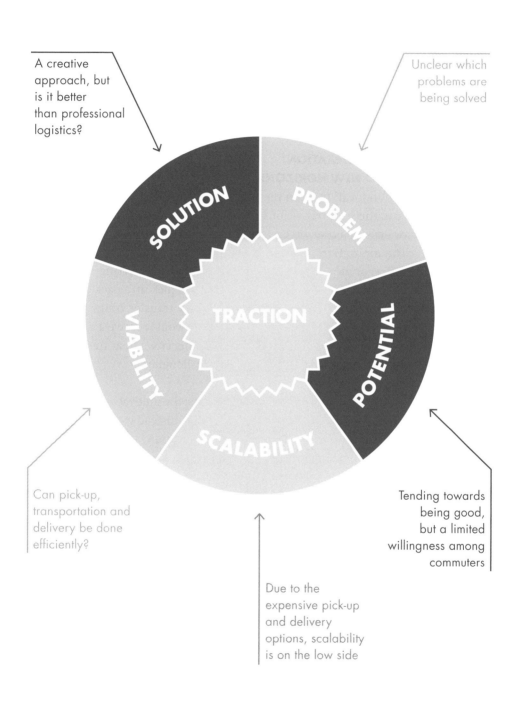

A creative approach, but is it better than professional logistics?

Unclear which problems are being solved

SOLUTION

PROBLEM

TRACTION

VIABILITY

POTENTIAL

SCALABILITY

Can pick-up, transportation and delivery be done efficiently?

Tending towards being good, but a limited willingness among commuters

Due to the expensive pick-up and delivery options, scalability is on the low side

THIRD ITERATION:
BACK TO ROUND TWO

Once again, the process was quick, and on making this valuable discovery, the innovation team decides to revisit their original idea of empty space once again, focusing on possible pivots. In their first iteration, they came across the owner of a bicycle courier company who complained about the couriers' wait times between deliveries. At the time, the owner had said, "This is dead time, and profit margins drop." Would changing the target group be a worthwhile pivot?

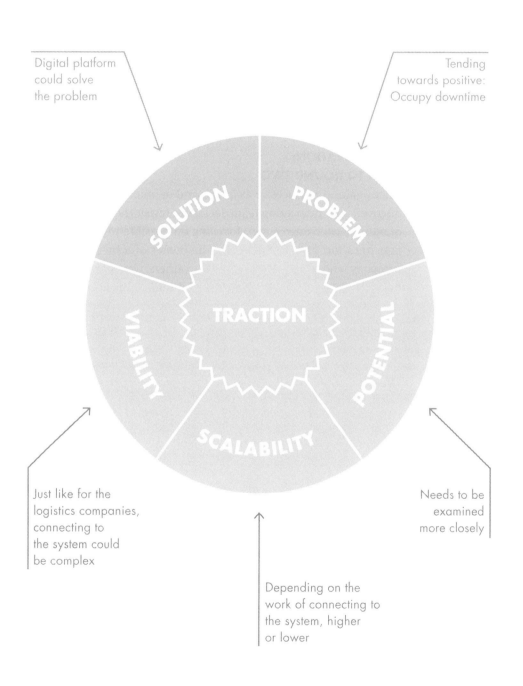

Digital platform
could solve
the problem

Tending
towards positive:
Occupy downtime

SOLUTION

PROBLEM

VIABILITY

TRACTION

POTENTIAL

SCALABILITY

Just like for the
logistics companies,
connecting to
the system could
be complex

Needs to be
examined
more closely

Depending on the
work of connecting to
the system, higher
or lower

FOURTH ITERATION:
ON THE TRAIL OF ENTHUSIASM

Their enthusiasm on the rise, the innovation team contacts the courier company to interview the owner. He seems really interested and asks if they can already take the solution with them and demonstrate it. This is a sign of enthusiasm. It seems as though the team has finally come across a truly relevant problem for which there is still no satisfactory solution. They pursue this now more promising approach and check first whether the idea is worth it in terms of potential, business model viability, and scalability. In particular, the innovation team needs to find out if the interested company represents a single case, or whether enough courier companies might be interested, The innovation train keeps rolling…

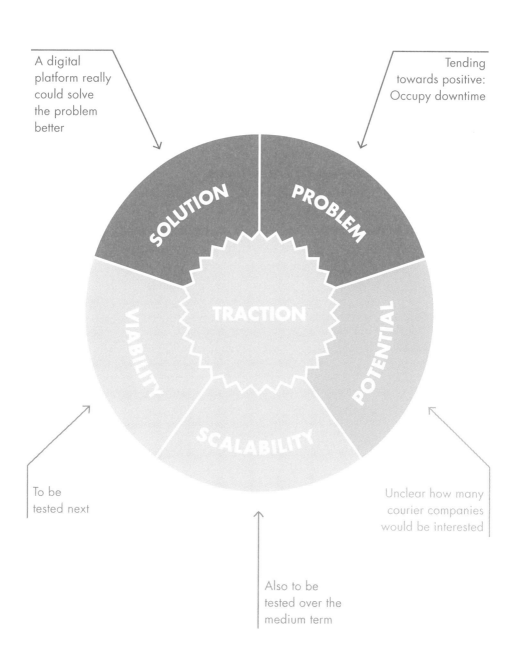

THE SEVEN INNOVATION PATTERNS

S tartup and innovation projects start with a variety of ideas, topics and intentions. The Lean Progress Model makes it apparent which success factors take center stage at the beginning. For example, many startup founders start with a concrete solution idea and only identify afterward which problem they're actually solving with it. But we also find problem solvers who first and foremost dedicate themselves to an exciting and important problem, and then look for a solution to it.

WHICH SUCCESS FACTOR DOMINATES THE PROCESS?

With the help of the Lean Progress Model, we can identify seven typical innovation patterns and types of innovators, which will be described in the pages below. Individual people, groups or even organizations can show certain tendencies towards preferred starting points. At the very least, projects preferably start by focusing on the respective success factor. Being aware of patterns like this helps guide the innovation process in a manner that is more transparent, quick, and successful.

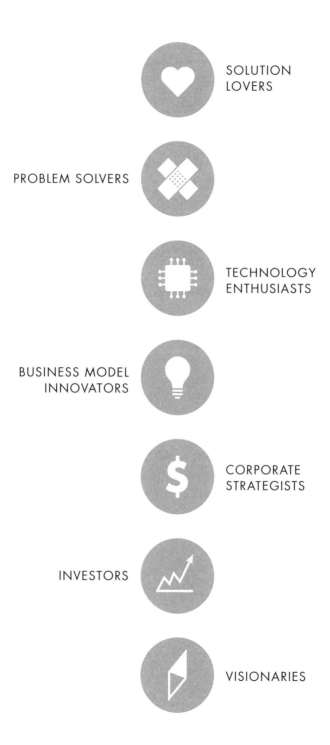

SOLUTION
LOVERS

PROBLEM SOLVERS

TECHNOLOGY
ENTHUSIASTS

BUSINESS MODEL
INNOVATORS

CORPORATE
STRATEGISTS

INVESTORS

VISIONARIES

Overview of the seven innovation patterns

INNOVATION PATTERN 1: SOLUTION LOVERS

Solution lovers usually start with a solution idea of which they're so convinced that they vehemently defend their idea and only make changes with great reluctance. The advantage of this is that they're not quick to get worked up by unconventional ideas and correspondingly critical feedback, which is certainly necessary for some ideas. On the other hand, flexibility in the discovery and learning process according to Lean is extremely important. There's the risk that solution lovers will waste unnecessary time and money defending their idea, without learning anything in the process. Only people who remain open-minded will quickly and easily recognize the path to success.

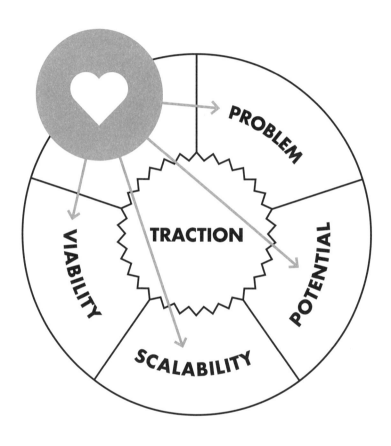

INNOVATION PATTERN 2: PROBLEM SOLVERS

P roblem solvers are actually the exact opposite of solution lovers. They've identified an exciting problem that they absolutely want to solve. If the potential customers also assess the problem as being truly relevant and feel it hasn't yet been adequately solved, the opportunity for added value is relatively high. Yet first, a worthwhile and truly better solution needs to be found, which isn't always easy. Sometimes, problem solvers don't have the creativity it takes to come up with solutions that are genuinely innovative. Problem solvers, by contrast, are much more flexible than solution lovers when it comes to changing the solution. In this respect, they have clear advantages from the perspective of the discovery and learning process according to Lean Innovation.

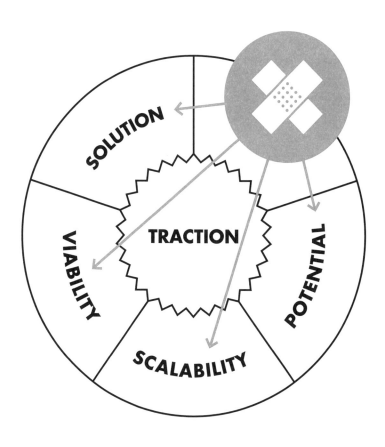

T echnology enthusiasts see a concrete technological innovation as having great potential for a startup or innovation
project. Either they've developed the technology themselves, as
engineers or inventors, and maybe they've already taken out a
patent on it, or they're so enthusiastic about a certain new technology and the related craze that they absolutely have to devote
their energies to coming up with an innovation in this field. For
example, technology enthusiasts might first dedicate themselves
to the new opportunities brought about by artificial intelligence
or biomedical engineering, and it's only in a second step that they
look for problems to be solved or concrete solutions.

INNOVATION PATTERN 3: TECHNOLOGY ENTHUSIASTS

For the most part, technology-related topics and the possible
problem and solution fields are very far-reaching and varied. In
this regard, technology enthusiasts are, from a Lean Innovation
perspective, similar to problem solvers in terms of flexibility,
provided they don't start with a concrete solution.

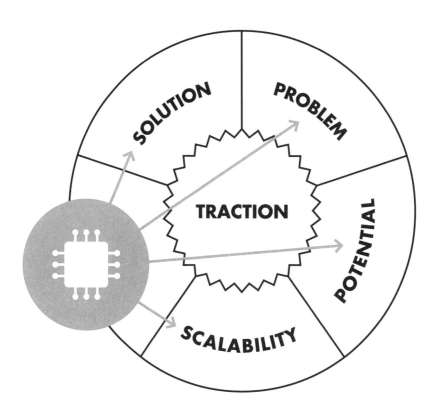

INNOVATION PATTERN 4: BUSINESS MODEL INNOVATORS

B usiness model innovators have identified the still too-seldom-used innovation and differentiation potential of new business models. Therefore, they first develop an innovative and promising business model. If they do this in a related field with a related offering, the business model innovation in the Lean Progress Model might only affect the viability, potential and scalability. But if an innovative product or service is to be produced, then naturally the product and the solution would also have to be analyzed and tested. However, as a rule, business model innovators put viability and the business model's potential for success first.

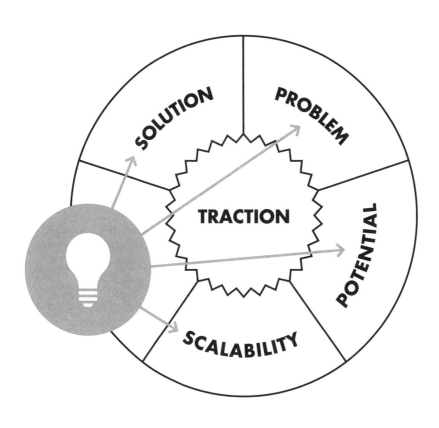

INNOVATION PATTERN 5: CORPORATE STRATEGISTS

C orporate strategists, as the name implies, are more likely to be found in established and larger companies. Their purpose is to safeguard the long-term success of the business by setting a strategic course and developing new business areas. For this reason, they have to pay close attention to correspondingly big and attractive potential. Which problems and solutions closely contribute to this is secondary. In many cases, several ideas are entered into the race and researched simultaneously, to increase the chances of harnessing potential. Corporate strategists are also more flexible in terms of changing ideas, provided the organization and the corporate culture permit these changes.

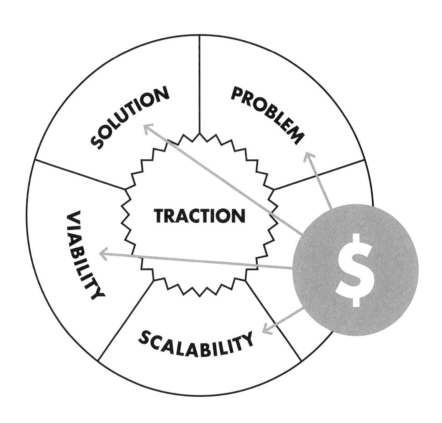

INNOVATION PATTERN 6: INVESTORS

A s a rule, external risk capital investors are interested in seeing all success factors for a new business idea assessed as positive (green) and that the success can be proven as very promising early on, according to the traction indicator. However, if it is about the basic assessment of an idea, even as compared to other ideas, the degree of scalability stands front and center. The more scalable an idea is, the higher the return on investment in the event of success. This is necessary so that the investment losses for all unsuccessful investments can at least be balanced.

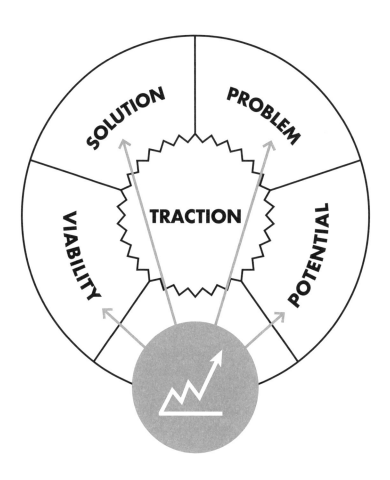

I nnovators who don't prefer a specific success factor are, in most cases, driven by a vision. A vision could be something like a major improvement to a traffic situation in city centers. This is neither a clear problem nor a clear solution. Various problems can be identified within this vision: the uneven distribution of traffic in the day-to-day, polluted air, or pedestrian safety. Very different solutions are conceivable for these problems. For example, to better distribute traffic: tolls in city centers at specific times of the day, or promoting public transit.

INNOVATION PATTERN 7: VISIONARIES

Visionaries have the advantage of being very flexible across a broad subject scope and are still focused on running the discovery and learning process according to Lean Innovation. Of course sooner or later, visionaries also have to decide on a specific problem and solution.

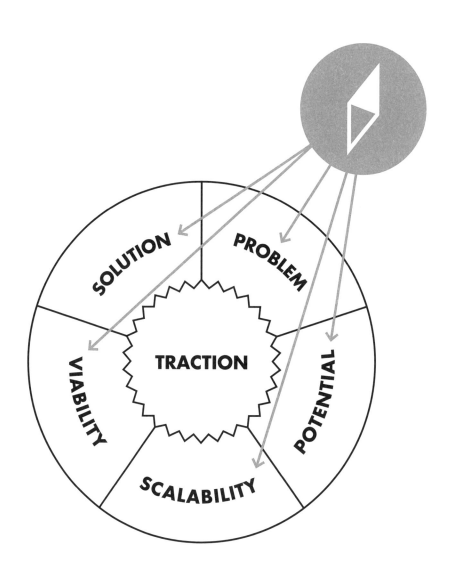

CONCLUSION

In a 2017 book, Lean paradigms are summarized as Sense and Respond.[58] The authors talk about <u>learning their way forward</u> to pave the way to innovation success and that a <u>continuous two-way conversation with the world</u> is required for this. What's fascinating about this description is that this forward learning actually represents one of the most natural things in the world, because we as people have always behaved this way, as has the environment. Maybe we in management will consequently return to our roots as human beings, who, through trial and error, understand and shape the world.

GOING FORWARD

One disadvantage of the sense and respond idea is that it could be passively interpreted because according to it, we first have to be aware in order to be able to react. But don't we have to take the wheel more often, even if, in the process, we are very open and flexible in our observations and reactions? To emphasize the active element, I'd rather talk about "creating and sensing." We each contribute an initial idea, an initial suggestion to the world and in return, we receive reactions. And in this way, we actively learn our way forward to pave the way to success.

In a similar manner, the book and the model were consolidated more and more through numerous conversations, interviews and experiments, until they became the book you are currently holding in your hands. Now I can't wait to find out what you, the reader, do with it. I'm looking forward to hearing about your exciting applications, ideas and suggestions:

E-Mail: david@leaninnovationguide.com
Social: linkedin.com/in/davidgriesbach
Newsletter: bit.ly/2MKxQ9p

CREATING

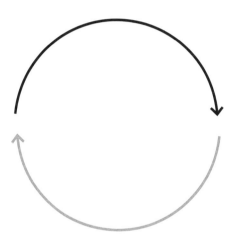

SENSING

Innovation as active learning forward

THANKS TO CONTRIBUTORS

The people listed here have contributed to the creation of this book and the model with their feedback, inspiration and constructive criticism.

Thank you immensely for your valuable support!

I also owe my gratitude to the Lucerne School of Business, which funded this book project with a financial contribution and is always open to groundbreaking management topics.

Lilit Aebersold
Urs Aeschlimann
Philipp Aeschlimann
Noemi Aggeler
Omar Al-Odeh
Furtuna Alaj
Mariya Alipieva
Lea Allemann
Fernando Ammann
Agatha Anthamatten
Daniela Apreda
Vicente Aranguiz
Aurasiri Arkarawanatorn
Manuel Aufdenblatten
Romy Bacher
Silvan Baumgartner
Kate Bayer
Suzan Bayrak
Danka Bekcic
Peter Berchtold
Raphael Berger
Claudia Bienentreu
Zsuzsa Bilato-Orosz
Andreas Bircher
Christoph Birkholz
Oliver Bissig
Carol Andrina Blumer
Youri Böhler
Emilie Boillat
Alexandra Bolliger
Jovana Bozic
Olha Brändli
Patrick Breiter
Azemina Brkic
Leandra Bruder
Daria Brühwiler
Markus Brun
Ronnie Brunner
Kilian Buck
Heidi Bühler
Tobias Buri
Oliver Bürki
Deborah Cadien
Roberto Caligiuri
Flurin Capaul
Miriam Christ
Dominik Cihla
Samira Courti
Domenica Crescionini
Alexandru Nicolae Cretu
Noemi Cuadra

Remo Dahinden
Michael Davis
Maxime Davis
Vanja Decurtins
Daniel Ehrensperger
Fabian Elmiger
Dominik Emmenegger
Stephanie Engels
Peter Erne
Michel Fernández
Michael Fischer
Nadine Fischer
Severin Frank
Mathias Frei
Andreas Frey
Alvaro Fussen
Alexander Fust
Jürgen Galler
Kiara Dalissa Galvan Reyes
Daniel Gasser
Rinaldo Gentinetta
Manuel Gerres
Luca Giacomelli
Fabienne Gisiger
Emilija Gjorgjievska
André Glutz
Svetlana Golovina
Prisca Götz
Rainer Grau
Gabriel Grob
Benno Häfliger
Andrea Häfliger
Cornelia Hauri
Claudia Heger
Boaz P. Heller
David Hengartner
Severin Hiltbrunner
Roman Hofer
Christin Hoffmeyer
James Holroyd
Philipp Holzherr
Isabella Holzmann
Doreen Hungerbühler
Laura Hutter
Noè Infantino
Florian Iseli
Michael Jäggi
Oliver Jeger
Alexander Joost
Tobias Jordi

Martin Kägi
Andreas Kälin
Stephanie Kaudela-Baum
Andy Keel
Peter Kels
Lukas Keusch
Tobias Kluge
Florian Knupfer
Anna Kobi
Sarah Koch
Karolin Köhler
Georgios Kontoleon
Kevin Kottmann
Michael Krähenbühl
Gabriela Krummenacher
Andreas Kubli
Vlastimil Kudrnac
Christoph Kuen
Basil Küng
Veronica Lange
Marion Lehmann
Anna Katharina Leu
Jana Lév
Stevica Levajkovski
Yue Li
Oi Yan Li
Manuel Lichtsteiner
Patrick Link
Kay Lummitsch
Florian Lussi
Barbara Lüthi
Philipp Lütolf
Martin Mächler
Karachach Madörin
Jan Maisenbacher
Sladjan Maksimovic
Marco Malinverno
Raphael Medici
Martin Meier
Silvan Meister
Marco Menotti
Larissa Mesmer
Tobias Mettler
Nicole Mieschbühler
Lars Minder
Cyril Mugglin
Björn Müller
Sinja Müller
Lukas Müller
Jörg Müller

Georgie Mutebi
Erik Nagel
Alfonso Navarro
Caitlin Nebroj
Raluca-Maria Nedelcu
Marija Nikolikj
Julien Nussbaum
Manuel Oberhänsli
Andreas Oberrauter
Guido Anthony Oswald
Karoline Otte
Cem Özbek
Hristina Pavlova
Dominik Perego
Lukas Peter
Abhijit Phondke
Prachi Rane
Manuela Rantra
Marc Reichert
Daria Reisch
Silvan Renggli
Stefan Rogenmoser
Noemi Rom
Ivo Ronner
Raphaela Rudigier
Lukas Rüdlinger
Katja Ruffiner
Nigar Rustamova
Ramon Rütimann
Afrodita Sadiku
Ligia Carla Sánchez Cárdenas
Rodolfo Santos Gomes
Fred Schaerlig
Sara Schaller
Katja Schaller
Sandra Scheibling
Emanuel Scherer
Martin Schmid
Jessica Schmid
Fredi Schmidli
Michélle Jacqueline Scholtz
Michael Schranz
Iris Schuler
Silvan Schuppisser
Dominik Schürmann
Beat Seeliger
Karim Shaanon
Shinthu Shanthakumar
Mariana Stankovic

Roger Steffen
Oliver Stein
Egon Steinkasserer
Ingo Stolz
Fabian Stoop
Christian Strong
Samira Suter
Luzia Suter
Christina Taylor
Miguel Saul Terrero Morillo
Oliver Thoma
Sonya Janelle Thormoset
Tobias Thurnherr
Andreas Tietze
Michael Tiziani
Martina Triulzi
Flavio Trolese
Jennifer Trowbridge
Aleksandra Tyankova
Marco Veri
Ricarda Vogt
Sophie von Falz-Fein
Adrian von Orelli
Dijana Vukicevic
Stefanie Wall
André Waller
Chengmin Wang
Dirk Weber
Laurent Weber
Tina Weilenmann
Selina Weingartner
Mario Wermelinger
Lea Wick
Désirée Widmer
Mike Woelfel
Hoi Ting Wong
Susi Wüst
Pascal Wyss
Selina Wyss
Flavio Wyss
René Zeier
Norbert Zeller
Markus Zemp
Marco Zemp
Maximilian Zimmermann
Marilena Zingg
Yuliya Zlatanova
Daniel Zumoberhaus
Stefan Zurflüh

END NOTES

1 Blank, S., & Dorf, B. (2020). The startup owner's manual: The step-by-step guide for building a great company. Hoboken: John Wiley & Sons

2 Maurya, A. (2012). Running lean: Iterate from plan a to a plan that works (2nd edition). Sebastopol: O'Reilly

3 Swisscom (2017): www.swisscom.ch/de/business/start-up/blog-und-events/blog/blog-2017-29.html; accessed on August 13, 2018; AXA Versicherungen (2015): www.axa.com/en/spotlight/story/ start-in-how-to-innovate; accessed on August 13, 2018; Rivella (2018): www.cin-cin.ch/unsere- aufgaben; accessed on August 13, 2018; Lufthansa (2018): lh-innovationhub.de; accessed on August 13, 2018; Kärcher (2018): productinnovationeducators.com/blog/tei-103-how-karcher-developed- a-new-product- that-captured-the-market-with-bill-ott/; accessed on August 13, 2018; Sennheiser (2016): www.youtube.com/ watch?v=d82TjAtzlvw; accessed on August 13, 2018

4 Schneider, J., Hall, J. (2011). Why Most Product Launches Fail. In: Harvard Business Review, 89(4), pp. 21–23.

5 Maurya, A. (2012). Running lean: Iterate from plan a to a plan that works (2nd edition). Sebastopol: O'Reilly

6 Blank, S., & Dorf, B. (2020). The startup owner's manual: The step-by-step guide for building a great company. Hoboken: John Wiley & Sons

7 The thirty to fifty interviews are to be understood as a benchmark. Naturally, it depends on how much we change a startup or innovation process in the Lean Innovation process. However, the author Cindy Alvarez uses fifteen to twenty interviews per hypothesis as the benchmark: Alvarez, C. (2014). Lean Customer Development: Build Products Your Customers Will Buy. Sebastopol: O'Reilly

8 Ries, E. (2011). The lean startup: How today's entrepreneurs use continuous innovation to create radically successful businesses. New York: Crown Business

9 Blank, S., & Dorf, B. (2020). The startup owner's manual: The step-by-step guide for building a great company. Hoboken: John Wiley & Sons

10 Schneider, J., Hall, J. (2011). Why Most Product Launches Fail. In: Harvard Business Review, 89(4), pp. 21–23

11 Maurya, A. (2012). Running lean: Iterate from plan a to a plan that works (2nd edition). Sebastopol: O'Reilly

12 Mobile Payment Startups: angel.co/mobile-payments, accessed on Apr. 6, 2018

13 Maurya, A. (2012). Running lean: Iterate from plan a to a plan that works (2nd edition). Sebastopol: O'Reilly

14 Osterwalder, A., & Pigneur, Y. (2010). Business model generation: a handbook for visionaries, game changers, and challengers. Hoboken: John Wiley & Sons

15 Maurya, A. (2012). Running lean: Iterate from plan a to a plan that works (2nd edition). Sebastopol: O'Reilly

16 Osterwalder, A., & Pigneur, Y. (2010). Business model generation: a handbook for visionaries, game changers, and challengers. Hoboken: John Wiley & Sons

17 For a detailed description, see: Maurya, A. (2012). Running lean: Iterate from plan a to a plan that works (2nd edition). Sebastopol: O'Reilly

18 Osterwalder, A., & Pigneur, Y. (2010). Business model generation: a handbook for visionaries, game changers, and challengers. Hoboken: John Wiley & Sons

19 Alvarez, C. (2014). Lean Customer Development: Build Products Your Customers Will Buy. Sebastopol: O'Reilly

20 SyncDev (2018). A Proven Methodology to Maximize Return on Risk: www.syncdev.com/minimum-viable-product/; accessed on Aug. 13, 2018

21 Wedell-Wedellsborg, T. (2017). Are You Solving the Right Problems? Harvard Business Review, 95(1), pp. 76–83.

22 Christensen, C. M., Hall, T., Dillon, K., Duncan, D. S. (2016). Know Your Customers' "Jobs to Be Done". In: Harvard Business Review, 94(9), pp. 54–83

23 Maslow, A. H. (1943). A Theory of Human Motivation. In: Psychological Review, 50, pp. 370–396

24 Eyal, N. (2014). Hooked: How to build habit-forming products. New York: Penguin.

25 Almquist, E., Senior, J., Bloch, N. (2016). The Elements of Value. In: Harvard Business Review, 94(9), pp. 46–53.

26 Almquist, E., Senior, J., Bloch, N. (2016). The Elements of Value. In: Harvard Business Review, 94(9), p. 52

27 Almquist, E., Cleghorn, J., Sherrer, L. (2018). The B2B Elements of Value. In: Harvard Business Review, 96(2), pp. 72–81.

28 See for example: jobstobedone.org/radio/unpacking-the-progress-making-forces-diagram/; accessed on July 2, 2018; see also: rossbelmont.com/post/90597943108/four-forces-of-product-switching, accessed on July 2, 2018, and blog.strategyzer.com/posts/2017/9/11/how-customers-adopt-products accessed on July 2, 2018

29 Fogg, B.J. (2009). A behavior model for persuasive design. In: Proceedings of PERSUASIVE'09

30 ibid.

31 Maurya, A. (2016). Scaling lean: Mastering the key metrics for startup growth. New York: Penguin

32 ibid.

33 Porter, M. E. (2008). The Five Competitive Forces That Shape Strategy. In: Harvard Business Review, 86(1), pp. 78–93

34 Blank, S., & Dorf, B. (2020). The startup owner's manual: The step-by-step guide for building a great company. Hoboken: John Wiley & Sons

35 Kaplan, S. (2012). The Business Model Innovation Factory: How to Stay Relevant When The World is Changing. Hoboken: Wiley

36 Osterwalder, A., & Pigneur, Y. (2010). Business model generation: a handbook for visionaries, game changers, and challengers. Hoboken: John Wiley & Sons

37 Basic idea inspired by Maurya, A. (2016). Scaling lean: Mastering the key metrics for startup growth. New York: Penguin

38 Maurya, A. (2012). Running lean: Iterate from plan a to a plan that works (2nd edition). Sebastopol: O'Reilly

39 Ismail, S. (2014). Exponential Organizations: Why new organizations are ten times better, faster, and cheaper than yours (and what to do about it). New York: Diversion Books

40 Gomez, P., Probst, G.J. (2007). Die Praxis des ganzheitlichen Problemlösens: Vernetzt denken – Unternehmerisch handeln – Persönlich überzeugen Bern: Haupt

41 Heath, C., & Heath, D. (2007). Made to stick: Why some ideas survive and others die. New York: Random House

42 Berger, J. (2014). Contagious: How to Build Word-of-Mouth in the Digital Age. London: Simon & Schuster

43 Parker, G. G., Van Alstyne, M. W., Choudary, S. P. (2016). Platform Revolution: How Networked Markets Are Transforming The Economy And How To Make Them Work For You. New York: W. W. Norton & Company

44 Ismail, S. (2014). Exponential Organizations: Why new organizations are ten times better, faster, and cheaper than yours (and what to do about it). New York: Diversion Books

45 Eyal, N. (2014). Hooked: How to build habit-forming products. New York: Penguin.

46 Salazar, C. (2013) under techcrunch.com/2013/04/22/want-to-raise-a-million-bucks-heres-what-youll- need/; accessed on August 14, 2018.

47 Maurya, A. (2016). Scaling lean: Mastering the key metrics for startup growth. New York: Penguin

48 Croll, A., Yoskovitz, B. (2013). Lean Analytics: Use Data to Build a Better Startup Faster. Sebastopol: O'Reilly

49 Weinberg, G., Mares, J. (2015). Traction: How Any Startup Can Achieve Explosive Customer Growth. New York: Portfolio / Penguin

50 With reference to the following quote from marketing pioneer John Wanamaker: "Half the money I spend on advertising is wasted; the trouble is I don't know which half."

51 Please direct licensing questions to license@leaninnovationguide.com.

52 Furr, N., Dyer, J. (2014). The Innovator's Method: Bringing the Lean Start-up into Your Organization. Boston: Harvard Business Review Press

53 www.cnbc.com/2018/03/07/snap-layoffs-engineering-team-said-to-see-up-to-10-percent-cut.html; accessed on May 28, 2018

54 www.uber.com/newsroom/company-info/; accessed on May 28, 2018

55 Doerr, J. (2018). Measure What Matters: How Google, Bono, and the Gates Foundation Rock the World with OKRs. New York: Portfolio/Penguin

56 Ries, E. (2011). The lean startup: How today's entrepreneurs use continuous innovation to create radically successful businesses. New York: Crown Business

57 Müller, R., Thoring, K. (2012). Design Thinking vs. Lean Startup: a comparison of two user-driven innovation strategies. Contribution for the International Design Management Research Conference 2012

58 Gothelf, J., Seiden, J. (2017). Sense and Respond: How Successful Organizations Listen to Customers and Create New Products Continuously. Boston: Harvard Business Review Press

REFERENCES

Almquist, E., Cleghorn, J., Sherrer, L. (2018). The B2B Elements of Value.
In: Harvard Business Review, 96(2), pp. 72–81

Almquist, E., Senior, J., Bloch, N. (2016). The Elements of Value.
In: Harvard Business Review, 94(9), pp. 46–53

Alvarez, C. (2014). Lean Customer Development: Build Products Your Customers Will Buy.
Sebastopol: O'Reilly

Berger, J. (2014). Contagious: How to Build Word-of-Mouth in the Digital Age. London: Simon & Schuster

Blank, S., & Dorf, B. (2020). The startup owner's manual: The step-by-step guide for building a great
company. Hoboken: John Wiley & Sons

Christensen, C. M., Hall, T., Dillon, K., Duncan, D. S. (2016). Know Your Customers' "Jobs to Be Done".
In: Harvard Business Review, 94(9), pp. 54–60

Croll, A., Yoskovitz, B. (2013). Lean Analytics: Use Data to Build a Better Startup Faster. Sebastopol: O'Reilly

Doerr, J. (2018). Measure What Matters: How Google, Bono, and the Gates Foundation Rock the World
with OKRs. New York: Portfolio / Penguin

Eyal, N. (2014). Hooked: How to build habit-forming products. New York: Penguin.

Furr, N., Dyer, J. (2014). The Innovator's Method: Bringing the Lean Start-up into Your Organization.
Boston: Harvard Business Review Press

Gomez, P., Probst, G.J. (2007). Die Praxis des ganzheitlichen Problemlösens:
Vernetzt denken – Unternehmerisch handeln – Persönlich überzeugen. Bern: Haupt

Gothelf, J., Seiden, J. (2017). Sense and Respond: How Successful Organizations Listen to Customers and
Create New Products Continuously. Boston: Harvard Business Review Press

Heath, C., & Heath, D. (2007). Made to stick: Why some ideas survive and others die. New York:
Random House

Ismail, S. (2014). Exponential Organizations: Why new organizations are ten times better, faster,
and cheaper than yours (and what to do about it). New York: Diversion Books

Kaplan, S. (2012). The Business Model Innovation Factory: How to Stay Relevant When The World is Changing. Hoboken: Wiley

Kirsner, S. (2016). The Barriers Big Companies Face When They Try to Act Like Lean Startups: hbr.org/2016/08/the-barriers-big-companies-face-when-they-try-to-act-like-lean-startups; accessed August 13, 2018

Maslow, A. H. (1943). A Theory of Human Motivation. In: Psychological Review, 50, pp. 370–396

Maurya, A. (2012). Running lean: Iterate from plan a to a plan that works (2nd edition). Sebastopol: O'Reilly

Maurya, A. (2016). Scaling lean: Mastering the key metrics for startup growth. New York: Penguin

Müller, R., Thoring, K. (2012). Design Thinking vs. Lean Startup: a comparison of two user-driven innovation strategies. Beitrag für die International Design Management Research Conference 2012

Osterwalder, A., & Pigneur, Y. (2010). Business model generation: a handbook for visionaries, game changers, and challengers. Hoboken: John Wiley & Sons

Parker, G. G., Van Alstyne, M. W., Choudary, S. P. (2016). Platform Revolution: How Networked Markets Are Transforming The Economy And How To Make Them Work For You. New York: W. W. Norton & Company

Porter, M. E. (2008). The Five Competitive Forces That Shape Strategy. In: Harvard Business Review, 86(1), S. 78–93

Ries, E. (2011). The lean startup: How today's entrepreneurs use continuous innovation to create radically successful businesses. New York: Crown Business

Schneider, J., Hall, J. (2011). Why Most Product Launches Fail. In: Harvard Business Review, 89(4), pp. 21–23

Wedell-Wedellsborg, T. (2017). Are You Solving the Right Problems? In: Harvard Business Review, 95(1), pp. 76–83

Weinberg, G., Mares, J. (2015). Traction: How Any Startup Can Achieve Explosive Customer Growth. New York: Portfolio/Penguin

INDEX

ABOUT THE AUTHOR

David Griesbach, Dr. rer. Soc. HSG (Doctor of Social and Economic Studies, University of Saint Gallen), *1977, is a Lean Innovation and Lean Startup expert. For his doctoral thesis, he developed an approach that already anticipated the important elements of Lean Innovation. For twenty years he has been consulting and supporting businesses and other organizations at the intersection between strategy and innovation. David Griesbach is also a lecturer at the Lucerne School of Business for the Master of Science and the EMBA program, among others, and gives introductory keynote speeches at events and for corporations.

www.davidgriesbach.com

ABOUT THE DESIGNERS

Equipo is a design studio for visual communication in Basel. Since its founding in 2007, they have worked in the fields of print and corporate design as well as designing interactive media. The company owners, Christian Heusser and Roman Schnyder, learned their craft at the Academy of Art and Design in Basel, which, in the 1920s, helped shape the so-called "Swiss Style," a tradition in typography and grapic design that continues to influence modern-day work. The owners of Equipo also lecture for the "Human Computer Interaction Design" Master's program at the Eastern Switzerland University of Applied Sciences and the University of Basel.

www.equipo.ch

LEAN INNOVATION TOOLS

The Lean Innovation Guide website is a knowledge platform where you can find a PDF of the poster for the Lean Progress Model and other tools.

www.leaninnovationguide.com

Subscribe to the newsletter and receive tips, tricks and tools on the topic of Lean Innovation:

bit.ly/2MKxQ9p